Issues in Defence Management

Issues in Defence Management

Edited by
Douglas L. Bland

SCHOOL OF POLICY STUDIES
QUEEN'S UNIVERSITY, KINGSTON, ONT.

Canadian Cataloguing in Publication Data

Main entry under title:

Issues in defence management

Selected papers presented at a symposium held at Queen's University, Kingston, Ont., spring 1997.
Includes bibliographical references.
ISBN 0-88911-811-6 (bound)   ISBN 0-88911-809-4 (pbk.)

1. Military administration – Congresses. 2. Canada – Armed Forces – Management – Congresses. 3. Military planning – Congresses.
4. Military planning – Canada – Congresses. I. Bland, Douglas L.
II. Queen's University (Kingston, Ont.). School of Policy Studies.

UB146.177 1998   355.6   C98-931424-3

© School of Policy Studies, 1998

Contents

	Preface	vii
	List of Acronyms	ix
1.	Issues in Defence Management: An Introduction *Douglas L. Bland*	1
2.	Reforming Defence Management: Lessons from the New Zealand Defence Force Experience *Cathy Downes*	13
3.	Managing Defence in the Post-Cold War Era: A View from the United Kingdom *Martin Edmonds*	33
4.	Distributing the Defence Budget: Choosing Between Capital and Manpower *John M. Treddenick*	57
5.	Education in Defence Resources Management: The Next Decade *John E. Dawson and Charles J. LaCivita*	83
6.	Military Educational Reform and Defence Management Studies in Hungary *Zoltán Szenes*	99
	Contributors	123

Preface

This book is a collection of selected papers presented at a symposium, *Issues in Defence Management*, held at Queen's University at Kingston in the spring of 1997. The meeting was organized to bring together scholars, officials, and military officers to consider the changes that are directing the ways and means of defence management in the post-Cold War era. Although the situation in Canada provided a focal point for the discussions, it was soon evident that many of the concerns facing defence managers in Canada, and elsewhere, cross international boundaries, extend beyond "alliance politics," and influence the policies and procedures of lesser states as much as they affect the major powers. There was, however, in this diversity, agreement on one issue — that the practice of managing resources for national defence has changed and will continue to change and that no new management paradigm appropriate to the circumstances of national defence planning has yet emerged to guide defence planners in the 1990s and beyond. Business planning and "re-engineering" alone will not do.

The symposium was made possible by the assistance and support of several individuals. I acknowledge the contribution of the Security and Defence Forum of the Canadian Department of National Defence. Marc Whittingham, Director of Public Policy, DND along with his staff helped to arrange the attendance at the conference of several senior officials from the department as well as officers of the Canadian Armed Forces. These individuals added greatly to the debates. Several individuals who presented papers that were not reproduced here and others who chaired plenary sessions made important contributions to the symposium. I would like to thank Dr. Peter Kasurak, Office of the Auditor General of Canada; Dr. Ernest Gilman, Ottawa; Professor Robert Bernier, École nationale d'administration publique, Université du Québec; Anthony Rustin, SNC Industrial Technologies Inc.; Major-General George Macdonald and Pierre Lagueux, both from National Defence Headquarters, Ottawa; and Dr. Jack Granatstein.

I would like to acknowledge the support of members of the School of Policy Studies, Queen's University who assisted this project. They include Lois Jordan, Assistant to the Chair in Defence Management Studies, who organized the symposium; Mark Howes, Valerie Jarus and Marilyn Banting, who carefully edited and produced this book.

I would also like to thank Professor Keith Banting, Director of the School of Policy Studies for his continuing support to me and the Defence Management Studies Program.

Douglas Bland
Queen's University
Kingston

List of Acronyms

DND	Canadian Department of National Defence
DoD	Department of Defense (US)
DRA	Defence Research Agency
DSA	Defence Support Agencies (UK)
FMI	Financial Management Initiative (UK)
FPMG	Financial Planning and Management Group
FYDP	Future Years' Defense Program (US)
GAO	Government Accounting Office (US)
HDF	Hungarian Defence Force
IMF	International Monetary Fund
JCS	Joint Chiefs of Staff
LTC	Long-Term Costings
MAXIS	Cost-Centre Accounting and Budget System for Administrative Expenditure (UK)
MINIS	Management Information System for Ministers and Top Management (UK)
MOD	Ministry of Defence (UK)
NAO	National Audit Office (UK)
NAPNOC	No Acceptable Price, No Contract (UK)
NCO	Non-Commissioned Officer
NZDF	New Zealand Defence Force
NMS	New Management Strategy (UK)

OPPRES	Operational Preparedness Performance Reporting and Evaluation System (NZ)
OMB	Office of Management and Budget (UK)
OSD	Office of the Secretary of Defense (US)
PCP	Program Change Proposals (to PPBS)
PPBS	Planning, Programming, and Budgeting System
RBs	Responsibility Budgets (UK)
RMA	Revolution in military affairs
RP	Resources and Programmes Staff (UK)
SECDEF	Secretary of Defense (US)
TLBs	Top Level Budget-Holders (UK)
UN	United Nations
ZMKA	Zrínyi Miklós War College

CHAPTER ONE

Issues in Defence Management: An Introduction

Douglas L. Bland

If the central defence management question during the Cold War was: "How much is enough?" the most pressing question today is: "How can we do more with what we have?" With only a few exceptions — the Republic of China, for example — soldiers and defence managers are asked to provide sophisticated military capabilities with less money, resources, and people.

Answering the question and selecting a strategy to maximize the outcomes of defence spending is made complicated in 1998 by several difficulties. During the Cold War many critical planning factors were known, sometimes in detail. Today, in a "threat ambiguous environment," the only element of national defence planning that seems certain is uncertainty. There is no enemy nor any opponents' grand strategy against which to build national armed forces. Theatres of operations in Europe, in the Atlantic, Pacific, and the Mediterranean Sea, and in the airspaces over North America once etched in the minds of generations of officers, appear almost irrelevant to those engaged in operations since 1989. Who would have predicted in 1988 that throughout the next decade the armed forces of the Western democracies would be engaged mainly in, and stressed by, conflicts in the Balkans, Africa, and the Persian Gulf?

The nature of warfare may be constant, a place, as John Keegan reminds us, of fear and bravery, boredom, and terror (Keegan 1976). However, the environment of warfare is changing and evolving rapidly in some technologically advanced states. The so-called "revolution in military affairs" (RMA) provides enormous advantages in combat on land, at sea, and in the air and it is transforming machine-age warfare. Nevertheless, the revolution is unevenly spread, even among modern states, because it is founded on unique combinations of technical, industrial, and managerial capabilities that in turn arise only in wealthy states with large, technically educated populations. On the other hand, the ever present contradictions of international relations and warfare may depreciate the assumed benefits of the RMA.

While advanced weaponry can dramatically reduce an opponent's machines and support facilities to rubble and lead to a quick victory, the same result is difficult to achieve when one is fighting an enemy whose strength is not dependent on machines. In Vietnam, Afghanistan, and Somalia the value of highly technical weapons and the forces built around them was problematic. It is not obvious that smart bombs can seek out fighters immersed in an innocent population. In such circumstances perhaps only the old-fashioned smart infantry will succeed. Indeed, the very success of the RMA in some states may spark a counter-revolution in "dumb weapons" and smart tactics in other states. Guerrilla warfare, "war in the shadows," is always available to those who cannot match the strength and technical capabilities of their enemy's mainline, modern forces.

Although weapons, forces, and other capabilities created by the RMA may be cost-effective because, presumably, they reduce the duration of wars and human casualties, they are, nonetheless, costly to build, maintain, and employ. States with limited funds for defence may not be able to afford such capabilities or if they are able to buy some limited quantities, the numbers may not provide much real advantage. Eventually, nations like the United States, which can afford to run with the RMA, may find that they are so far in front of their friends and allies that they, out of necessity, become the champions of all. They may find themselves also saddled with the responsibilities and challenges that leading demands. Allies, on the other hand, may find themselves dragged into expensive defence programs or strategies that they would otherwise avoid. The long-term influence of the RMA on allied politics and defence management is not yet clearly evident.

Citizens and politicians in most states that have endured the high costs of the Cold War expect some relief, "a peace dividend," from the end of that conflict. Who would deny that the vast store of weapons, forces, defence industry, and infrastructure accumulated between 1950 and 1989 is now, in some respect, redundant? The difficulty is determining just what is redundant; is it weapons or forces, industry or infrastructure or some combination of all these resources? If a reduction in expenditures is worthwhile, where does one begin to make the necessary cuts? Should states lop off the top of the structure or chop away at the bottom? Are reserves more cost-effective than forces-in-being? Should governments spend money on readiness for current operations and missions or direct defence funds to research, the defence industrial base, and recapitalization of capabilities to construct a viable future force? How this particular question is resolved could turn the present force into the enemy of the future force or the future force into the enemy of today's readiness.

How can we get more "bang for the buck" and make do with what we have? These are questions at the centre of defence policies worldwide. Obviously, these are not questions that can be answered only by throwing money at them. Many ideas that once provided a framework for decisionmaking and resource allocations are now wanting. Politicians, military officers, and defence bureaucrats are searching for a new conceptual framework and new ways to manage national defence so as to preserve and build capabilities relevant to the needs of the post-Cold War world. This book is a collection of views on the nature of defence management and ideas for the way ahead in 1998.

DEFENCE MANAGEMENT

It is sometimes convenient to segregate strategic and tactical operations from defence management, if only to simplify the study of warfare and national defence. The two fields, of course, cannot be bounded or separated in practice and must be considered together. Defence management, to paraphrase Henry Eccles, "is the bridge between the economy of the nation and the tactical operations of the combat forces. Obviously, then the [defence management] system must be in harmony, both with the economic system of the nation and with the tactical concept and environment of the forces" (Eccles 1965, p. 72).

At the level of governments, defence management transforms national policy into activities and joins the agencies of the state and the national economy to the armed forces, usually through some type of defence ministry. From this perspective, defence management is embraced by the national facts of life and concerned with civil-military relations, national economics, and domestic politics, along with the organization and functions of government. At a second level, defence management is about transforming allocated resources into military capabilities relevant to and in accord with government policy. Managing the national defence, therefore, requires a policy base, instruments and organizations to perform various and special functions; and individuals appropriately trained in defence science, defence economics and finance, law, industrial relations, and government.

The reality of bureaucratic politics and the vested powers of military officers and officials are too great to simply declare defence managers squires to combat commanders. Choosing between different ways to achieve defence outcomes is the essence of defence management at senior levels of government and the power of managers — whether politician, soldier, or public servant — lies in the discretion they have to choose among alternatives. In government, considerable bureaucratic power often flows to advisers who make the choice of possible options for politicians. Defence management, therefore, "is concerned with political responsibility, not the outpouring of menial clerks"(Sweetman 1984, p. 4). It is part of governance and the policy process that defines problems and chooses solutions to address them.

ISSUES FOR TODAY

The papers in this study address three critical issues facing defence managers (and commanders) in 1998. If defence management is about choosing how to administer policy and how to convert resources into military capabilities, then the instrument for choosing, the defence ministry, is of primary concern. Ministries of defence on the Western model, which combine the responsibilities and authorities of politicians, bureaucrats and military officers are, in the long history of warfare and government, relatively recent innovations. They provide effective ways to join governments and armed forces and allow for the legitimate interplay of the three principal groups that make up the defence establishment. Although the Western model of an integrated ministry of defence has been a success (and is the NATO-standard organization in all member states and a near perquisite for states seeking membership), it is by no means a perfect instrument for managing national defence.

Ministries of defence can become bloated, stultified organizations seemingly concerned more with form than function. The integration of soldiers and civilian bureaucrats is not easily accomplished, nor do such arrangements exist for long without serious friction caused by fundamental differences in interests, perspectives, and attitudes.

Most ministries of defence combine the political and bureaucratic offices designed to support civilian ministers of defence with the senior command elements of the armed forces, but the fit is usually roughly forced together and uncomfortable. The greater the friction and discomfort, the less likely the chance that political, military, and public service leaders will find an operating consensus to guide defence management. In the absence of a consensus on policies on issues such as the roles and missions of the armed forces, the size of the defence budget, the organization of forces and the terms of reference for ministers, officers and bureaucrats, the ministry might become an arena for internal sparring and not a bridge from which to steer the national defence effort.

FINDING EFFICIENCIES IN ORGANIZATION AND METHODS

Governments have been forced recently to look at their ministries of defence in order to find ways to improve their efficiency while consolidating the successes of the integrated model. Cathy Downes examines defence management "down under" in her paper "Reforming Defence Management: Lessons from the New Zealand Defence Force Experience." Admittedly, New Zealand has a small defence force with limited capabilities, but these limitations are a bonus for researchers in the sense that they simplify elements of the discussion on defence organization without detracting from essential considerations. Downes first situates the New Zealand Defence Force (NZDF) and the defence reforms in the context of a wider government strategy to change "the business practices of the nation." The NZDF was caught up in attempts by government to stimulate the competitiveness of the private sector by releasing it from regulations and encouraging initiatives intended to bring "commercial disciplines" into public administration machinery.

The business plan approach to defence management developed in the NZDF has been a qualified success. According to Downes, a cooperative political-military system for determining "outputs" and gearing them to budgets and audits has enabled the NZDF to deliver "nearly the same quantity and quality of outputs as ten years ago but for approximately two-thirds of the price to New Zealand taxpayers." However, the business plan approach as applied to defence management is not without problems, mainly because defining military outputs is so difficult.

New Zealand politicians tried to free themselves from the tyranny of their experts by both forcing a separation between those responsible for providing policy advice and those responsible for administering policy, and by adopting what they called "contestable advice." The notion was that ministers only have true freedom to decide when they are provided with independently evaluated advice. This concept led them to separate the Ministry of Defence from the NZDF. In this regard, New Zealand ran counter to the trends in most other states where ministries have become increasing integrated, if not unified. Cathy Downes explains that the concept and the structure that flowed from it have not prospered well.

"Efficiency" is an elusive term, especially as it applies to the armed forces in war and peace. In recent years in many states, the quest for efficiency seems to overrun military demands for effectiveness in warfare. Martin Edmonds explores this contraction in his survey of defence management in the United Kingdom over the last 20 years. In "Managing Defence in the Post-Cold War Era: A View from the United Kingdom," Edmonds, like Downes, places defence management in a government and social context. He emphasizes that not only must military affairs follow the dictates of policy, but defence policy and the armed forces must be managed in accordance with general rules and norms applicable to all government departments. Senior officers in the United Kingdom can no longer look to the special nature of national defence for relief from frugal governments and their management gurus.

Edmonds reviews the various reasons for the drive toward efficient defence — a changed international situation, the high cost of weaponry, the desperate state of British finances, and "Thatcherism," among other things. He next traces the management strategies tried by ministers, noting their successes and failures. Politicians in every department attempted, generally, to separate policymaking from implementation. This notion and the icon of efficiency became policy in the Ministry of Defence based on the assumption that bureaucratic efficiency would produce improved and effective defence capabilities. Although the broad aim to improve management and "good housekeeping" was readily achievable, it was never easy for officers and officials to demonstrate an exact link between this effort and improved national defence.

Over the years, several new ideas and methods were introduced by ministers. These included, for instance, the development of quasi-official defence agencies to manage important policies and functions; the contracting-out of many activities; and the delegating of control (and risks) to lower level officers and officials.

The United Kingdom has a unique (and for foreigners, a sometimes baffling) system of defence organizations at the centre that depend on a subtle process of consensus-building through committees. It has worked reasonably well in the past, but the system in the 1980s soon attracted attention because it appeared overly redundant and layered in conflicting authorities. These observations led to recommendations to integrate further the ministry and the high command, "to break down organizational boundaries between services," and to create more or less permanent "joint" headquarters to encourage and facilitate interservice cooperation and the coordination of policy and military operations.

In the past 20 years the British armed forces have been reduced by up to a quarter of their Cold War strength, inventories of weapons have been cut back, and the national defence strategy has been changed to meet new threats and demands. Defence budgets have steadily declined in real terms. Politicians, officers, and officials have sought to accommodate these changes by finding ways to do military things more efficiently. However, the danger, as Edmonds explains, is that efficiencies created in response to peacetime pressures might not withstand the demands of war. "The longer term benefits, or costs, of [these] practices have still to be established." Although efficiencies may drive out redundancies, cautious people of experience know that "redundancy is a necessity, not a luxury, in war." The lingering question for the efficiency managers is always, "will it work in wartime?" Martin Edmonds, for one, is not so sure that anyone knows the answer or even if it has even been adequately considered.

THE ECONOMICS OF NATIONAL DEFENCE

The efficient allocation of scarce defence resources among competing demands is a permanent issue for political leaders and defence planners. Governments and defence ministries have tried various methods and techniques to determine defence needs and to make rational allocations such that resource distribution just matches requirements. Most of these *rational systems* are of limited value and fail to explain adequately the workings of the *actual process* that allocates resources over time. That actual process is complicated by its high political content, the uncertainties in international relations and warfare, and by the inescapable struggle for resources between the interest groups that make up the armed forces.

Understanding the actual process is also complicated because arguably there are several allocation processes in play at any time in most defence bureaucracies. For instance, there is a continual competition between national policy components, between "guns and butter." There are competitions within the defence and security communities between foreign aid and development funding and military funding. Within the defence establishment there are struggles between the services and inside the services for particular programs, clashes between military officers and civil servants, and skirmishes between the guardians of the official process and bureaucratic opportunists. From a macroeconomic point of view, there are ongoing competitions between the main components of defence spending, personnel, operations and maintenance, and capital. Finally, perhaps, there is always a contest between the champions of force readiness and force development. Despite these complexities, defence managers cannot ignore the allocation dynamic in defence planning.

John Treddenick at the beginning of his paper, "Distributing the Defence Budget: Choosing Between Capital and Manpower," highlights the importance of the allocation problem. "It is no exaggeration," he explains, "to suggest that how the budget is allocated is as clear a statement about a country's defence posture as is the size of the budget itself, perhaps even more." In Treddenick's view, defence allocation is "a two-stage economic process." First, governments decide the level of the defence budget and then defence managers decide how it is to be spent. In this sense, policy follows from budgets and from internal allocations of that budget.

Treddenick, a defence economist, considers an aspect of the allocation dynamic, capital versus manpower, as a way of thinking about the larger question of the internal distribution of defence dollars. He wishes to know, generally, what is the appropriate distribution of funds? Treddenick situates the question in the Canadian experience and employs some "basis economic ideas ... to clarify the nature of the problem of choosing between capital and manpower." The model he develops for this purpose helps to draw some inferences about how to make choices and the consequences of taking different allocation decisions.

We might assume that the goal of defence management is to produce an optimum defence capability from the resources provided for national defence. This simple equation, however, disguises several critical aspects of defence planning.

Should one begin the planning process or analysis at the point of inputs — government allocations — or at the opposite end, at the point of outputs? Outputs, however, can be merely the residuals of inefficient, and thus ineffective, allocation processes; one driven by domestic political imperatives, for instance. It might be more useful to manage defence policy and spending on the basis of precisely defined (and in New Zealand, contracted) outcomes, various categories of capabilities, and to place those objectives foremost in the allocation process. Treddenick then "forces us to come to grips with the concepts of defence outputs and defence inputs" in the context of the allocation dynamic.

EDUCATING THE MANAGERS

Who needs to know what? This is a fundamental question before every educator. National defence is managed at various levels and degrees by politicians, military officers, and public servants. Most, but not all, of these individuals reside within the defence establishment, broadly defined. Nevertheless, defence managers, especially at the centre, function within a wide government environment and without perfect control over their actions and decisions. Generally, therefore, we can assume that military officers and officials are the "target audience" for defence management educators. (There seems to be little hope of formally educating politicians in defence management, except through the sometimes painful process of "internal briefings" and personal experience.)

Determining what managers need to know is more problematic. Should they, for example, be completely indoctrinated in the formal techniques for defence decisionmaking (whatever those may be in the state in question), or should they be educated so they can adapt to the bureaucratic politics of defence management? How is one to incorporate into a defence management curriculum all the ancillary subjects that a well-rounded officer or official needs as background information in the daily job? Defence managers should know, for instance, something of politics and government, organizational and decisionmaking theories, international relations and warfare, law, ethics, and economics. Is there a field of study called defence management having its own conceptual framework, literature, and history and how does it (if it exists) differ from public administration and business management? Is knowledge of defence management transferrable between states and cultures? This question is particularly germane today as Western liberal democracies attempt to spread their concepts and styles of government to so-called emerging democracies and defence partners.

Two papers in this volume address aspects of these questions. John Dawson and Charles LaCivita meet the current education challenge head-on in their paper, "Education in Defence Resources Management: The Next Decade." According to the authors, defence management is caught up in a "major shift in attention by executives in the public sector." This shift is causing the "strategic process" to become "more periodic" while the "operating process" is becoming "more immediate." Governments are increasingly concerned with "performance" and being "where the action is." The accumulative effect of downsizing, restructuring, and flattening of organizations allows (or demands, perhaps) the close management of policy and administration by senior officers and officials. This new environment, in the opinion of Dawson and LaCivita "calls for a change in emphasis in education in resources management."

They begin by reviewing the development of defence resources management from the end of the Second World War to the fall of the Berlin Wall. The system developed during this period (mainly in the United States and the United Kingdom) called for officers and officials who had backgrounds in economics, decision science, and management systems theory. Moreover, officers and officials assigned to work within the resources management process required training in cost-benefit analysis, systems analysis, and program management.

The "current environment" is not as urgent as the previous Cold War period. Defence decisionmakers in most areas have been given an opportunity to step out of the arms race and the continuous scramble for new and better capabilities. Today, they can take a "periodic approach to the big issues" in an atmosphere that gives "greater stability to the defence program." However, this respite is not a "stand-down" from operations, because it is characterized by ongoing low-level operations, as in the former Yugoslavia. While time and opportunity exist to rethink fundamental issues and to reorganize the armed forces, "the message [is that] defence management has to continue to operate the 'going store' while changing how the store operates."

The authors illustrate how this new emphasis on operations and change is borne out in major innovations in defence resources management. Defence managers now need to know not only the techniques particular to their special area, but they also need to be much more acquainted with businesslike practices, production economics, human behaviour, and how organizations change. The bottom line for Dawson and LaCivita is that defence management education needs to aim at producing officers and officials who can work in the periodic and immediate world of change, reform, and consensus. This new emphasis does "not require radical or wholesale departures from the way defence resources management have been taught in the past." But it does require "a modest shift that gives more attention to operations and less to weapons acquisition." Teachers and scholars of defence management, however, do face a major challenge and that is to develop ways to explain the underlying rationale for the defence management systems and techniques that are emerging in a radically different post-Cold War era.

Few citizens, politicians, officers, or officials in any state confront a greater challenge than those in the emerging democracies in Eastern and Central Europe who are trying to change the political and military culture of their armed forces. Officers in these states must not only become acquainted with a vast range of foreign (in all senses of the word) political, social, and military concepts, but they must submit to a fundamental reorientation of the way they think about armed forces and society. And they need to learn quickly.

Moreover, defence planners in Eastern and Central European states were told by domestic and allied politicians to build ministries of defence like those in Western states. However, leaders there had no more than a dim comprehension of a ministry of defence as Westerns understand the term. Moreover, Western ministries depend on large numbers of specially trained and experienced public servants, but in 1989-90 few of the new partnership and allied states had any defence public servants capable of moving into high office. Misunderstandings, lack of information and experience, and the practical difficulty in finding suitable public servants for defence ministries produced additional stresses on military officers and civil-military relationships in these states.

The need to reeducate the officer corps and establish a viable defence civil service is almost an overwhelming task for reformers in Eastern and Central Europe. Nevertheless, they, with assistance from NATO and member states of the Alliance, have made some notable strides in this direction. Zoltán Szenes, a general officer in the Hungarian Defence Forces, is both an example of the changes that are possible and an influential advocate for reform. In his paper, "Military Educational Reform and Defence Management Studies in Hungary," Szenes explains the changes and the frustrations that move hand-in-hand through this sentinel period in Hungarian history. He reminds us that defence management, like defence policy and the character of a state's officer corps, is built on the social, cultural, political, and military history of the state. Each system is, therefore, unique and one should expect that they can graft a foreign defence structure onto a living organism without accommodating local circumstances.

Szenes reviews the disputes over fundamental political and military reforms that in some cases continue to worry those trying to change the military education system in Hungary. There were many disputes; and how current agreements will fall out in the future is not obvious. Army officers had to build a national armed force from the remnants of their Warsaw-Pact-dominated military. They had to reconcile themselves to civil control by politicians few trusted or respected. Budget cuts and the demands of new NATO "partners" forced officers to learn new languages, modern marketing methods, Western-style terminologies and techniques, all while meeting the sometimes unrealistic demands of politicians for immediate change.

In the midst of these problems, a dispute erupted in 1990 concerning the reform of higher education of the officer corps. Politicians wanted to use civilian standards in the new system but senior officers resisted, insisting that military norms prevail. Concern for the details of officer education in this context became a second-order question after consideration of who would control this type of basic national defence policy decision. Szenes outlines the argument (it continued for three years) and how the Hungarian Defence Forces finally accepted a "defence university" concept for higher education and enacted laws to support the change.

The Hungarian Defence Forces, like armed forces in most modern states after the Cold War, had to decide what and how to teach officers. The essential difference for Hungarians was that they had to reform officers' education in the midst of unprecedented social and political change. The professional debates, familiar to Western military officers, focused on the degree to which senior officers must be educated in subjects, like defence management and government, that are outside a strictly military curriculum. Szenes explains these arguments and the outcome of the often intense debates. He follows this overview with a detailed description of the current state of officer education in Hungary.

DEFENCE MANAGEMENT FOR THE FUTURE

The symposium on *Issues in Defence Management* that brought the authors of this study together was intended to touch on some of the issues facing politicians, military officers, and officials who manage national defence during this period of significant change. There are many such issues and, indeed, issues within issues, but defence organization for decisionmaking, resource allocation, and the education of managers are important building blocks in any national defence system for management.

Although the practice of defence management is the usual fare in discussions and writings in this field, policies and practices are really "ideas in action." Therefore, studies of the concepts underlying policy and practices ought to engage scholars and managers at least as often as management techniques and business procedures. For example, defence managers aim to develop efficient military capabilities that serve national defence policy effectively. The two concepts, efficiency and effectiveness, are key ideas in defence organization, economics, and education because a national defence system must function in peace and war where circumstances are usually always different. A cardinal objective is to develop defence management systems that are efficient in peacetime and effective and applicable without change in wartime. How is this to be accomplished?

Readiness is another basic concept, but what does it mean? Ready for what — for deployment or employment? Might it not be more helpful to assess the fitness of individuals, commanders, and units for operations? The idea of readiness is a critical element in defence management, but it is used and abused so freely that in practice the idea may have no meaning. Similarly, many states base defence allocations at the governmental and bureaucratic levels on rough notions of outputs, but this term also has "weak legs." Defence managers need to understand clearly what they are supposed to accomplish. Perhaps the idea of outcomes where that term means the coherent and comprehensive description of capabilities that include all materiel, personnel, training, and sustainment resources related to a capability would better guide the practices of defence planners.

Theory founded on valid concepts provides a beacon for safe passage in uncertain waters. Theory can never direct decisions, but it can help "to penetrate to the inner structure of warfare, to its component parts, and to their interrelations"(Eccles 1965, p. 27). Defence management in 1998 is in want of theory. Perhaps now, during the respite offered by the post-Cold War era, is the time to construct a conceptual framework on which to build a defence management theory for the future.

REFERENCES

Eccles, H.E. (1965), *Military Concepts and Philosophy*. New Brunswick, NJ: Rutgers University Press.

Keegan, John. (1976), *The Face of Battle*. London, UK: J.Cape.

Sweetman, J. (1984), *War and Administration: The Significance of the Crimea War for the British Army*. Edinburgh: Scottish Academic Press.

CHAPTER TWO

Reforming Defence Management: Lessons from the New Zealand Defence Force Experience

Cathy Downes

A PARABLE

There once was a small company. It had been in business for over a hundred years. It had a good reputation for delivering quality perishable goods to a few far distant customers through good times and bad. Costs were kept down by focusing on a specialized range of products where environmental advantage could be leveraged. The firm was run by monopoly boards set up for each product type under the broad control of a central head office that managed a range of other businesses. Because of a guaranteed market and a long period of consistent demand, the company's management felt that its resources could be diverted into improving both the welfare of its workers and the sharing of work among as many people as possible. Over time, work and management practices and investment and borrowing strategies became set against the achievement of these internal goals.

Inwardly-focused, the company failed to detect key signs of change. In a comparatively short time, the guaranteed market disappeared. Other larger and powerful producers could offer a broader diversity of products at cheaper prices. The borrowing strategy of the company had left it exposed when the costs of energy increased unexpectedly and dramatically. Management responded by instituting ever tighter internal controls. Capital needed to be borrowed to subsidize continued domestic production and the welfare of workers. More capital was borrowed to fund large projects to make the company self-sufficient in energy. To meet interest and loan repayments, the company was forced to freeze workers' wages and increase imposts upon them.

By now the company was one of the most heavily regulated in business. Management believed it could "control" its way out of the crisis or at least cushion the company from the effects of the crisis and hope for better times. However, this strategy only made things worse. The trading position of the company deteriorated and investors increased their interest rates or looked elsewhere. The company was speeding toward the precipice of bankruptcy at an alarming pace.

A new management team in 1984 faced the reality that radical change was no longer a scenario reserved for some management weekend seminar. Past strategies of minor tinkering with practices and plans so as to avoid hurting workers and their families was no longer feasible. Either the company dug itself deeper into a pit with rock bottom only inches away or it dug itself out. There could be no question that the only way to survival lay in accepting and enacting radical, rapid, and painful changes. The margin between survival and death was so small that management, shareholders and workers accepted that only through such change could the company hope to dig itself out of its difficulties and survive into the future.

THE REAL WORLD OF NEW ZEALAND IN 1984

Parables are grounded in the truth of a "real-world" situation. They are the case study generalized so that lessons can be learnt by those who have not experienced the true real-world situation. The lesson of this parable is that this is New Zealand's experience between 1984 and 1996 — for the company is New Zealand (NZ). How it has attempted to dig itself out of the pit which had been made for it, and to which it had so handsomely contributed over the years, is a lesson that others may wish to heed. Moreover, it is important to realize that the parable and the lesson are not over.

Because of the radical nature of change and its effect upon every sector of the New Zealand life over the period 1984-96, there is a natural need to breathe a sigh of relief and to congratulate itself for a job well done. However, New Zealanders (and not all) are only slowly and reluctantly accepting that the actions and changed directions of 1984-96 did not dig the country out of the pit, but did stop us digging a deeper grave and lifted the country off the bottom. These actions provided governments and both public and private sectors with the tools to continue the climb. It is a hard and unpalatable truth, but we will always be climbing out of the pit because the nature of the pit itself keeps changing.

This last in itself is a lesson that is still not understood by many businesses and institutions. Change completed is only the preparation for change to come. How many times have we all heard the phrase "change is constant"; the "only certainty is change," etc. Yet many people still accept reality only in rhetorical terms. It is only natural. People who endure a period of radical change where painful consequences appear early, and positive results are slow in coming — never matching ever-escalating expectations — want a period of "peace," of stability, of pause, and of rest. Unless coaxed to continue, this period of rest becomes so valued that the conditions are created by neglect that will demand yet another period of painful change.

The experience of reforming defence management must be situated within this broader context of New Zealand's economic and national management predicament and steps taken to work through it. This context is crucial for understanding how achievements were accomplished. To this end, this paper looks at the context of New Zealand's economic and national management reform program launched by the newly-elected Labour government in 1984 and carried on by its successor National Party government in 1990. It then examines how defence management was reformed within this context. Finally, the paper offers some observations and comments on the management, leadership, and organizational aspects of reform processes.

REFORMING THE BUSINESS PRACTICES OF A NATION: NEW ZEALAND 1984-1996

Democratically-elected governments need to find a careful balance of popular and "right" actions to take while in office if they are to underwrite their chances of staying there. It is almost one of Murphy's most agonizing laws of politics that few popular actions are right and few right actions are popular. However, in 1984, the newly-elected Labour government confronted a set of economic realities (ever-growing trade deficits, overwhelming debt levels, poor debt-equity ratios, protected, padded and inefficient industries, rampant inflation, poor returns on investment from investment-hungry state industries) that closed off popular choices of action, leaving only the right but definitely unpalatable ones. While some room for squirming existed, it is to their credit that the Labour government decided to stop searching for the path of least resistance and most electoral popularity. They took up a range of untried non-traditional economic and public sector management concepts and perspectives and initiated a sweeping and radical reform program that involved all sectors (public and private) of the economy, government itself, and all sections of New Zealand society. While gaining a second term in office in 1987 (with a much reduced majority) it continued with follow-on reforms which were, in turn, built upon by the further reforms of the National Party government elected in 1990.

This reform program had four powerful drivers — economic stress, failed government responses, new political leadership, and new ideas. Allen Schick, of the University of Maryland, remarked while reviewing the New Zealand state sector that "if any of these conditions had been missing, reform probably would have been modest and piecemeal" (1996, p. 11). It is perhaps the second lesson of the parable: real reform can only be effectively launched and boldly pursued if there is no clear alternative, if quite different ways of doing things can be identified, if new people come forward with energy and moral courage (or existing actors can be reinvigorated with both) and actors have legitimacy and unfettered power to take action.

The New Zealand reform program had three broad goals:

1. the removal of impediments, controls, and protectionism that had thwarted or discouraged the competitiveness of the private sector in international markets;

2. the redesign and rationalization of government's role in commerce; and

3. the building of a state sector that used commercial disciplines to generate directed levels of goods and services efficiently for the New Zealand people.

In terms of the first goal, the New Zealand dollar was devalued and subsequently floated. Controls on foreign exchange dealings were abolished. A wage/price freeze of the early 1980s was lifted. Controls on external investment, borrowing, and interest rates were removed. Foreign direct investment rules and entry barriers to banking were liberalized; so too were the Stock Exchange rules. Import tariffs were progressively reduced. A whole range of agricultural and consumer subsidies were abolished. A broadly-based consumption tax was introduced and previously punitive income and sales tax rates were reduced (NZ, State Services Commission 1996, p. 5).

By 1986, the NZ government had also prepared and launched a program to privatize, commercialize, and deregulate its involvement in commercial activities. Over time, governments had accumulated commercial businesses to supply much-needed national infrastructure and utilities — roads, railways, port facilities, electricity generation, and supply systems. This was followed by a second phase of business acquisition in order to broaden the base of New Zealand's economy by buying into and supporting industries that could not be sustained by the investment resources of New Zealand's private sector.

However, with no commercial incentives to discipline business practices, these industries had become inefficient, unresponsive, and sink-holes for investment, generating limited or dysfunctional results. As one commentator remarked: "state trade organisations handled 20% of the total investment of New Zealand, yet they only produced 10% of the country's output and every one of them made a loss" (Prebble 1996, p. 4). National employment was distorted and costly to taxpayers. Prebble went on to say that "the Railways and other state-owned organisations helped to employ people who would not otherwise have a job. Every artificial job in the Railways cost ten in the private sector. We know that every surplus job created in the coal industry cost the taxpayer $150,000 and the average over the rest of the trading departments was $75,000" (ibid., p. 33).

In 1986, the government passed the *State Owned Enterprise (SOE) Act*. This Act brought about a fundamental change in how SOEs were managed and regulated. Under the Act, such enterprises were to function as commercial enterprises. To this end, managers would be given the authority to control and manage inputs. Enterprises would be expected to pay tax and dividends to the government as returns on government investments as the shareholder. The aim was to make SOEs as efficient and profitable as comparable businesses not owned by the state. Bureaucratic deregulation, giving managers the authority and resources to manage, and setting in place firm and powerful accountability and performance mechanisms had a transforming effect.

For example, in the early 1980s, New Zealand Post lost millions of dollars a year, despite the fact that the cost of postage had been rising faster than inflation. Moreover, only about two-thirds of letters posted were delivered on time. By 1995, New Zealand Post was considered one of the world's leading postal services. Over 99 percent of letters to local destinations are delivered on time. In that year, the cost of stamps decreased by 10 percent with the government receiving some $84 million in tax and dividends that year. In 1987, US transport consultants Booz, Allen and Hamilton assessed NZ Rail as highly inefficient. By 1995, the World Bank was describing Transzrail as the world's most efficient railway. The managing director and others on his staff are recognized worldwide as innovative industry leaders. It should be noted that these managers were not commercial imports, but had worked for NZ Railways when the department was one of the world's worst (ibid., pp. 25-35; NZ, State Services Commission, p. 11)!

There was also a major rethink about whether or not the state should be in certain business activities at all. There was no strong evidence to suggest that social good was really protected by the state owning some types of businesses. Some businesses lacked the capital to develop as efficient enterprises and this capital could only be generated by greater government borrowing. And there was clear evidence that state-owned businesses were using capital already invested in them to only marginally achieve social goals. As a consequence, a broad spectrum of state-owned enterprises and assets such as Air New Zealand, forests, and telecommunications were partially or fully sold.

Between 1988 and 1993, the New Zealand government obtained $13 billion from these sales (State Services Commission 1996, p. 9). The overwhelming bulk of the revenue generated from these sales was devoted to reducing national debt levels. As a consequence of using the revenue for this purpose, with additions contributed from annual budget surpluses that began to be generated in the early 1990s, sufficient national debt has been retired to generate a 32-percent reduction in the debt interest charges being paid by government. Some businesses were only partially sold off with the state retaining a shareholding in increasingly successful commercial ventures. For example, in 1995, through its 49.9-percent equity stake in Telecom, the government received NZ $167.4 million in one half-year period alone.

While these reforms generated positive and enduring results, they were not achieved without cost, particularly in social terms. As feather-bedded state industries were sold off, significant numbers of make-work jobs were abolished as new owners introduced new technologies, retrenched unproductive business units and amalgamated units to achieve economies. In an economic sector where social goals rather than economic efficiency had dominated, isolated and small communities had developed around a single major industry that provided "government-guaranteed-jobs-for-life." When these industries were commercialized, there was no diversified base of industry to absorb redundant workers. Equally, services in isolated areas were reduced because the population base was insufficient to make servicing commercially viable. For a significant period of time — over a decade — unemployment rates rose before new industries and opportunities emerged and unemployment has fallen from a high of over 12 percent of the labour force to stabilize between 6-7 percent in the late 1990s.

Commercialization also revealed the extent to which uneconomic manually-intensive work practices had distorted the real need for low-skilled and semi-skilled workers. Newer employment opportunities increasingly require a re-skilled and up-skilled workforce and a system of education and qualifications capable of generating such a workforce.

The third key plank of government reform throughout the 1980s and early 1990s was reform of the remaining non-commercial core of public sector departments. The New Zealand public sector had developed along civil service principles of the British Westminster parliamentary system. It functioned through a unified, centralized, and common set of rules governing the provision of policy advice to government and the appointment and long-term development of career public servants. Pay, conditions, and promotions were all controlled through a central body — the State Services Commission. There was little possibility of lateral recruitment and rewards were targeted at long service and loyalty. If the State

Services Commission controlled public servants, the Treasury used its rule-making power to control the behaviour of public service departments. Over time, bureaucratic systems of rules and practices calcified. Management was reduced to incrementally adjusted baseline budgets expressed in input terms. Parliament, government and departments could not and did not realistically focus on what should be and were the results of expenditure. Department heads who sought to improve the efficiency and effectiveness of their departments were often thwarted by this web of rules and controls and bottom-up approach.

In 1988, the Labour government passed a crucial piece of legislation — the *State Sector Act*. This was followed in the next year with the *Public Finance* and *Reserve Bank Acts*. These three Acts have radically changed not only how public service departments function, but have fundamentally altered the whole concept of a public service. The key ideas of this concept are outlined in Figure 1.

FIGURE 1: Concepts of Management for Public Sector Departments

- Managers must have the freedom to act, to run their organizations free of *ex ante* control by outsiders (managerial discretion).

- Central control of inputs warps managerial behaviour and makes accountability of performance impossible.

- Policy advice and service delivery should be separated.

- Wherever feasible, contestable means of providing advice should be used.

- Where feasible, service delivery should be transferred to a tier of non-public service quasi-private and private sector organizations.

- Centralized controls should be removed from public service managers, while making them directly accountable for the performance of their organizations.

- Financial management systems should focus on purchase of relevant goods and services (outputs) rather than control of inputs.

- Departments must use full resource cost budgeting and accounting systems (accrual rather than cash management).

- Department heads are chief executive officers and employing authorities in their own right.

- Relationships with ministers is managed through annual departmental purchase agreements and CEO performance agreements.

Under the *State Sector Act*, the public service, as a unified organization, almost overnight ceased to exist. Each departmental head was invested with the responsibility and accountability of a business chief executive. As a consequence, department CEOs now are vested with authority for almost all input decisions — pay, appointments, organizational structures, production methods and systems, etc. Department CEOs negotiate an annual purchase agreement with ministers for the delivery of specified outputs for an agreed price. How (in terms of inputs and processes) these outputs are produced is the management responsibility of the CEO.

Under the *Public Finance Act*, new financial management systems were introduced to change radically the standards and transparency of financial performance in government departments. Departments were given just over a year to transit from cash accounting to accrual accounting methods, including assets registers and balance sheets.

Under the Act, departments are required to meet the same standards of financial management performance as are businesses. A capital charge is now levied on the value of each department's physical and financial assets minus liabilities. Departments have the ability to maintain and manage their own bank accounts. They may earn interest on these accounts. Budgets include a component for matched to depreciation of the existing asset base. From this component, departments are expected to repair or replace worn or obsolescent assets for which a continuing need can be proven. Only in exceptional cases are departments able to secure additional capital to fund capital projects. In such cases, an additional capital charge is levied on the department to reflect the cost of capital — in much the same way as interest on a house mortgage (Schick 1996, pp. 2-3).

THE EXPERIENCE OF REFORM

The period 1984-94 is already recognized as a decade of national revolution for New Zealand. According to Allen Schick:

> In budgeting and financial management, employment and human resource management, modes of appropriation, use of internal contracts, and other tools of management, New Zealand has ... revolutionized public management without going through the protracted pilot testing and cautious implementation that have slowed innovation in some other countries. Measured by their bold objectives, conceptual basis, reliance on statutes and speed of implementation, the New Zealand reforms have been truly remarkable (ibid., p. 2).

Revolution is never easy or pain-free. It must uproot and rip away the old in order to build the new. This is the nature of revolution. Moreover, it means going forward when the way is not clear and having first torn up the old ways of doing things. For people with no power over the changes that affect their lives, revolutionary change is both frightening and traumatic. Often such people hit out at the changemakers. As a consequence, for revolutions to work, they require revolutionaries with sufficient moral courage to pursue radical change. With only their self-belief in real success in a murky future they must confront and absorb severe personal reprobation and carpeting by the many who are affected by change.

Quite frequently moral courage is aided by necessitude. In New Zealand's case, the economic crisis of 1984 meant that there were few, if any, status quo options remaining. "No option but change" although grim and painful, could be used to convince the reluctant. Furthermore, the cushioning effects that successive governments had tried to achieve had left a New Zealand public with a high level of dependence upon government "omniscience." As a result, the revolutionaries were able to use the authority of their mandate to the fullest effect to push through unpalatable but necessary change.

It is a rare democracy that can effect revolutionary change. Indeed, it could be argued in New Zealand's case that public acquiescence was a crucial factor in allowing the revolutionaries to act boldly. Despite the significant improvements that have been achieved in putting the economy and the nation on a positive growth and survival path, the trauma associated with these changes is what the New Zealand public remembers and sees as a betrayal of their trust in a beneficent government. This perception of betrayal mobilized an apathetic public to reactionary activism that aimed at controlling public leaderships and ensuring that the revolutionaries would not gain ascendency again. This was reflected in the New Zealand public supporting, by the narrowest of simple majorities, the adoption of a new electoral system. Based on proportional representation, it almost guarantees that no one political party can gain a mandate to govern independently of other parties in a consensus coalition.

DEFENCE MANAGEMENT REFORM

The New Zealand Defence Force (NZDF) has participated in the full spectrum of the 1984-94 public sector management reforms. Following a major review of defence organization in 1989, the management of defence was divided into two separate government organizations — a civilian Policy Ministry of Defence, staffed by public servants, and a New Zealand Defence Force made up of a military force and a civil staff. This was confirmed in the *Defence Act* of 1991. Under the Act and the *State Services Act*, a civilian secretary of defence is responsible for the provision of policy advice to the minister of defence, the auditing and assessment of Defence performance and the acquisition of major capital equipment for the NZDF. For his part, the chief of the defence force (CDF) is the principal military adviser to the New Zealand government. He has responsibility for the operation of the NZDF, for contributions to policy development, and has sole financial responsibility and accountability for the overwhelming bulk of all defence funding. He is an employing authority in his own right, responsible for the pay, conditions of employment, and careers of the civil and military personnel under his command.

The NZDF has adopted accrual-based accounting and budgeting systems and has developed the full suite of management documentation (assets register, balance sheets, etc.) required of any business. As with other departments, it has an annual purchase agreement with its minister for the delivery of outputs specified in quality, quantity, and cost terms. It is the responsibility of the CDF with the support of his three chiefs of staff to determine how and what activities should be undertaken to deliver these agreed outputs. Throughout the defence force, there has been a comprehensive devolution of financial management responsibilities and accountabilities to formation, base and unit commanders. This has aligned spending and action responsibilities across the NZDF.

Over the last ten years, there has been a significant rationalization of infrastructure and commercialization of activities that do not need to be carried out by personnel in uniform. This has released resources for addressing core activity needs. A program of ongoing assessments of activities has been instituted to determine other commercially-focused ways of undertaking non-operational activities.

The NZDF has developed a unique set of concepts for specifying outputs that are relevant and meaningful in defence activity terms. Unlike most other government departments the critical product of the NZDF is a potential rather than actual capacity to deliver a result. In the NZDF's case the output is the potential capability to carry out selected military operations that when performed are likely to contribute to the achievement of the New Zealand government's strategic objectives. The set of performance delivery concepts reflect the dynamics that the defence force does not fight and win wars every day in the same way as a hospital does cataract and hip-replacement operations, or a library lends books. It is therefore necessary to reflect both the potential achievable capability that government can expect and the actual level of capability that is delivered on an annual basis.

Also unlike other government departments, when those results are delivered, the NZDF is unlikely to be the sole producer in both peace and war circumstances. In peace, it is an active partner with the Ministry of Foreign Affairs and Trade in promoting and protecting New Zealand's security interests. In almost all military operations to which NZDF units or personnel could be committed, it is anticipated that such operations will be combined or in coalition with the armed forces of other nations. As a consequence, separating out its output from that of any other contributor is difficult, and defining how much is enough to achieve government's security objectives is just as difficult.

This concept of actual and potential capability is unique to the Defence Force. It seeks to make transparent to the government that it is only purchasing a "maintenance" level of capability on an annual basis and the level of capability needed to carry out the peacetime engagement and deterrence and conflict prevention components of New Zealand's defence strategy. When the government activates any particular unit of the NZDF, that unit needs to be taken to an operational level of capability for the particular assigned military task. This can usually only be achieved and sustained with additional resources. The time taken to achieve an operational level is a risk calculation to minimize annual resource needs, but still have the military capability available to the government only when it needs it. In accepting the delivery of lesser levels of capability on an annual basis, the government formally accepts the lead-times and resource implications of activation of a capability.

In an overall sense, Defence has comprehensively embraced the package of public sector management reforms. Significant management efficiencies and improved management performance has been generated. It has undergone significant downsizing in terms of the personnel required to deliver the same outputs. This has been done at a time when the NZDF has had significant increases in its operating and personnel tempos with units being deployed overseas on UN and other operations. The NZDF has been able to take advantage of commercially-sensible business practices which were unavailable to Defence under the pre-1984 regime. These have reduced the resources needed to deliver the same outputs. Since 1990 saw a complete shift in the basis for budgeting from inputs to outputs — it is not possible to compare pre-1990 and post-1990 departmental performance. However, in broad terms, the contemporary NZDF delivers nearly the same quantity and quality of outputs as ten years ago but for approximately two-thirds of the price to the New Zealand taxpayer.[1]

LESSONS OF REFORM

Many significant results for the NZDF have flowed from this decade of management reform. One such result is a number of lessons on managing the reform process itself and on the consequences and implications of particular reforms. Some of these ramifications were unanticipated and not always valuable.

One-Size-Fits-All

Tenets of revolution state that it must be universal, change must be taken up by all, reactionary enclaves are a threat to the long-term durability of the revolution, and they constitute precedents that offer the unwilling an opportunity to backslide. Yet by the very nature of the diverse activities that revolution affects, it is inevitable that the "one-size-fits-all" approach will not fit all equally well. For those parts of the New Zealand economy and state sector that are, or approximate, commercial enterprises, the 1984-94 package of management reforms made business sense. The reforms were consistent with existing organizational culture, or involved an empowering cultural change that could be easily taken up by managers and staff alike.

Yet for some core government departments, the nature of their "product" does not lend themselves naturally to working through a commercial manufacturing, profit-loss dynamic. For these departments, the one-size-fits-all approach has made implementation of management reforms difficult, but not unworthy. It has meant that the fit is not perfect, but it has not meant that the garment should not be worn. At least this has been the experience of the NZDF.

This is particularly the case with the definition of Defence outputs. Each government department has had to evolve concepts for defining their outputs within broad parameters established by the New Zealand Treasury. Outputs must reflect the products delivered by the department, not a statement of how the department is organized, or of the goals trying to be achieved by the department. Outputs must be consistent and homogeneous in describing goods and services. They must specify quantity, quality and cost deliverables in terms that are measurable so that resultant performance can be audited and accounted for.

These parameters aim at presenting government with consistent and commonly-framed information from all departments. With this information, the government is better placed to make informed purchasing decisions between the goods and services of each department on an outputs, rather than simply a comparative cost basis.

As described above, the NZDF does not deliver goods and services on a daily basis. Rather, it delivers potential capability. As a consequence, it has been necessary to define a set of delivery concepts that are broadly consistent with the commercial logic being applied to all government departments, but which do not distort military operational dynamics and the effective processes and organizations for generating and sustaining military capability.

Appropriate output concepts must be matched by relevant concepts of performance measurement that are also militarily meaningful and meet auditing standards and principles. Performance measurement concepts must also be designed with an eye to integrating measured performance with expended resources, that is, linked financial and non-financial performance. It is only when there is a sound linkage between the two that department managers are able to use delivery performance concepts on an in-year basis to manage the most effective distribution of resources to achieve results.

For Defence, this has not been an easy task. Over a period of eight years some four different approaches have been applied; each seeking to better reflect the broad Treasury parameters required of Defence. The evolved outputs regime has been matched with a performance measurement system — the Operational Preparedness Performance Reporting and Evaluation System (OPPRES) — for measuring the delivery of Defence outputs from front-line force elements. OPPRES is shortly to be joined by a second measurement system designed to measure the delivery of internal outputs from Defence's support and overhead units that feed forward as inputs to the front-line force elements.

Defining outputs effectively is a central component of the overall management reform effort; and other key management changes hinge upon setting out a stable and meaningful expression of outputs. For example, until outputs are meaningfully specified, it is not possible to set in place appropriate cost attribution rules, because all organizational costs should be attributed to the final deliverables out of the department. If information systems are to efficiently record and attribute costs, they too must be designed against cost attribution rules and the final outputs.

Contestability of Defence Advice

A key aim of government reform was to separate policy and implementation and where feasible have contestable policy advice offering the government choices in its decision making. In Defence's case, this was to be organizationally achieved through the 1989 separation of the Ministry of Defence from the NZDF. While a sound concept in general theory, contestable advice, particularly areas of complex government activities, only has real utility when ministers have independent staffs to evaluate and interpret the merits of different advice for their minister. In the New Zealand parliamentary system, ministers do not have major independent staffs to carry out this function.

Moreover, in defence, it quickly became apparent that it was nonsensical to have an organization responsible and financially accountable for delivering policy results over which it had no influence. Moreover, because of the military and international security affairs dimensions of defence activity, high quality policy advice could only be derived from an integration of both military and civil inputs. Within a year of the reorganization, it was evident that contestability did not generate timely and valuable advice, but rather promoted contention, mistrust, and paralysis.

Over the 1990s, the two departments have attempted to evolve ways of integrating their work practices in those areas of activity where there is a legally established requirement (albeit that statutes are not particularly clear in their definition of responsibilities, having been drafted on the theory and not the practice of how these responsibilities needed to interact) for them to work together to achieve results. For example, new "joint" structures and a committee for bringing together the inputs of the two departments have had to be instituted.

In a era of vibrant commercial management reform, there is a growing awareness that a firm's critical advantage flows from the extent to which it can build relationships of trust, shared and common vision, and teamwork within its workforce. In seeking to achieve an improved result in high quality policy advice with options and choices for government decision making, the method chosen to achieve this result in Defence's case has worked against establishing and reinforcing these key relationships. This has handicapped the overall effectiveness of the organization.

Government's Ownership and Purchasing Roles

In a business sense, the government is both customer and shareholder of public sector departments. It owns the departments, and purchases goods and services from them. However, in business, most customers are not the controlling owners of a firm, particularly of large and multifaceted operations. This combination of roles is not always harmonious with ownership and purchasing goals differing and being in conflict with each other.

In the original reform conception, the central emphasis was on operational efficiency and accountability. This has led to a crucial stress upon the purchasing relationship between government and departments. In this, it has been highly successful. However, it resulted in reinforcing a governmental focus on short-term deliverables, with less attention being paid to the underlying infrastructure and manufacturing plant needed to sustain delivery over the long term. The stresses of this relationship are simply that of the future vying for equal consideration with the present in decision making, of maintaining and sustaining a capacity to deliver services in the future, just as much as actual contemporary delivery. For governments it also concerns the practical length of their long-term vision.

An attempt has been made to balance more effectively this relationship, particularly under the National and Coalition governments of the 1990s. There has been a conscious attempt to formulate a set of overarching strategic outcomes that are long term in nature, involve the long-term capacity of government departments to deliver outputs and extend to the end of or beyond a government's electoral term of office. Such outcomes are a cornerstone for developing an ownership perspective on public sector resource allocation. However, while such outcomes and responsive plans have been broadly defined, there is still an inherent preoccupation with short-term deliverables. There are significant consequences for the long-term infrastructure and the capital plants of departments. This can be seen, for example, in the disincentives inherent in the financial rules applied to capital projects.

In theory, setting aside funds annually, which approximate a level of depreciation of existing assets in order to fund replacements is sound. To accomplish this, departments are required to set aside depreciation capital funds at rates fixed by Treasury. These rates, however, do not always reflect the life or risk of the assets that would apply in the commercial world. Moreover, to encourage operational efficiencies, departments have received cuts or freezes in funding levels. In such circumstances, if more funds need to be set aside for depreciation because of the introduction of new assets, the funding must be found from that component of the budget for delivering outputs. This sets in place disincentives to capital investment in the first place.

If the assets' register of a department was set up at a time when the bulk of the department's assets were nearing the end of their life, the annual depreciation set aside would be low as was the case with Defence. With inflation (and particularly in Defence, military technology-driven inflation and in New Zealand, the lack of defence acquisition economies of scale) this means that there is a high probability that the amount of depreciation funding set aside will not be sufficient for the procurement of replacement or alternative assets. As noted above, if capital injections are required, a charge is levied on the capital to reveal the true cost of money. As with depreciation funding, capital charges must be met from the remainder of a department's funding allocation. If there is no agreed change in the levels of outputs to be delivered, funding for sustaining and generating capability into the future can be greatly handicapped (Schick 1996, pp. 53-62).

These issues are intensified for Defence, where the planning horizon for government's strategic outcomes (tailored to a three-year term in office) is far shorter than the planning-budgeting-acquisition-commissioning cycles for major defence equipment and capabilities.

Managing Reform Processes

The process that New Zealand Defence has gone through to implement public sector management reform initiatives itself reveals some important lessons. These are sufficient in themselves to warrant a separate paper. However, one lesson concerns the personnel needed to effect reform.

As observed above, revolution requires tearing up the old in order to find space for the new. It means dispossessing the power structures of the status quo and replacing them with power structures that suit the new. In personnel terms, management reform (both in government and private sectors) has most often involved downsizing and rationalization of a business' or department's workforce. There is no doubt that efficiencies have been achieved through "cutting out" managerial layers and through using technology to replace labour. Yet there are a number of side effects of personnel rationalization and its timing.

Reform is people-intensive. Machines do not create new processes. Computers do not evolve new business practices. Fax machines do not convince, persuade, inspire, and lead the adoption of those processes and practices. Yet in order "to create space" for reform, staffs are reduced in size to meet rationalization goals; many of those who remain are disempowered; they are tarred with the brush of being part of the old organization. Enter, stage left, the saviour of reform managers — the management consultant; a "bargain at the price" because they do not come with the "baggage" of current employees; they will do the job and go once it is finished.

However, in terms of building trust, of developing effective innovating teams, of giving and accepting responsibility, as a general rule, the management consultant is a negative force. At a time when those who have not lost their jobs are being expected to take salary cuts or freezes because budgets are being externally constrained, bringing in high-priced consultants who have no commitment to the organization sends a strong message which is hard to contradict: the staff feels that they are "not good enough" at their jobs, that new talent is needed. For some this may be the case. For others, it signals sufficient rejection for them to reject the organization and leave for better employment elsewhere. For most it will signal a lack of trust and commitment by the department or company's leadership.

For long-term and enduring management reform that builds effective staff participation, there can be no clearer message than that given by Charles Handy, (management researcher and philospher), to "check your management consultants at the door, you are the most qualified people to solve your own problems" (1995).

A second lesson of defence reform has been the need to resist attempts to treat defence uncritically and arbitrarily as a business. It is not a business and even the nearest analogy — to an insurance company — can lead to distortions and consequences which may only be revealed in future military operations; when lives, property, and national reputations are at risk. This does not mean that Defence, as a department of state, should be exempt from achieving high standards of operational efficiency and accountability. It means that best-business practices must be carefully evaluated in light of military operational conditions and requirements that are ultimately not set by national governments, but by opponents and allies.

A third lesson concerns the nature of goals set for reform initiatives. In some departments and companies, reform has been viewed as a "once-off" — there is a problem to be fixed and every effort should be made to find the very best solution and institute it. Then matters can return to normal, until something else breaks and another "fix" is needed. When change becomes a bit hectic and stressful, it is necessary to take a pause and allow people to catch up. This has been described as the "calm-lake" conception of change.

The alternative vision of change is more akin to white water rapids. In this conception, there are no calm lakes. There is only a tumult of river rapids of change. Companies and departments can only stay afloat and swim by focusing on achieving effective, but not always perfect, reforms. As Sir Winston Churchill once remarked, "perfection is spelt paralysis." In the white water rapids of change, to hold up all else until the perfect reform is completed can be a recipe for disaster. In seeking the perfect reform, the nature of the problem that generated the requirement for reform could itself change, thereby invalidating the particulars of the reform. In this context, the former chairman of the US joint chiefs of staff, General Colin Powell, has recommended that if zero is no solution and 1.0 is a perfect solution, act when you have achieved a 0.8 and be prepared to defend it (Roth 1993). In pausing to rest, the company or department risks being overtaken by change. It also risks allowing those staff who have no ownership over reforms to "opt out," to gather arguments and reasons for resisting change.

DRIVERS OF REFORM

Significant reform is the result of a number of drivers. In New Zealand and the NZDF, there were three such drivers (Schick 1996, pp. 11-19). First, an economic crisis of such magnitude that stability and incremental options for change could be discredited early and easily by reformers. The importance of invalidating such options should not be underestimated. The presence of crisis was used to overcome the reluctance of people to "move out of their comfort zones." The presence of crisis had a universalistic effect. It allowed government leaders to insist that no group, no department, and no sector should be exempt from reform. This constituted a powerful impetus for government departments, particularly those who had in the early 1980s struggled to institute reforms internally. Following 1984, government-wide reform was mandated. Following the *State Sector Act* of 1988, leaderships in all government departments were given freedom from over-regulation and a direction for reform. This combination of sectorwide freedom and direction was significant in motivating internal reform processes in each department.

The second driver was a change of government that brought into executive power a group of politicians prepared to act as revolutionaries and who would search out and find their counterparts in the public and private sectors. This group had the moral courage and self-belief to drive through initiatives that they believed were needed but which could bring, in the short term, only discomfort and difficulties for many people, and only in the longer term bring positive pay-offs. Even in the 1950s, Senator John F. Kennedy recognized the kind of moral courage needed by democratically-elected politicians to enact such reforms in a media age:

> Today the challenge of political courage looms larger than ever before. For our everyday life is becoming so saturated with the tremendous power of mass communications that any unpopulated or unorthodox course arouses a storm of protests ... And thus, in the days ahead, only the very courageous will be able to take the hard and unpopular decisions necessary for our survival (1964, p. 43).

The third driver of reform was the existence of new and alternative concepts of best practices and management principles. Knowing that an existing state is unsatisfactory is insufficient in and of itself to generate effective reform. It is the easiest task to criticize a current situation. It is the most difficult task to identify practical actions of change that have a reasonable probability of generating significant improvement. It is also a difficult task to convince both decisionmakers and followers that, although it is not possible ahead of time to specify in detail all aspects of a reform initiative and exactly how it will work and with what results, they should sign up and commit to it.

These three drivers — unifying crisis, morally courageous and independent "revolutionaries" in national and business leadership positions, and the availability of new ideas, rather than new and rehashed criticisms — are crucial in achieving significant reform. Many international reviewers of New Zealand's decade of reform have particularized the event. It is suggested that such reform initiatives could only have happened in New Zealand because of its small size and unique economic circumstances; that this invalidates such reforms for larger states and institutions. This view often seems to be used by those who are trying to avoid reform in the management practices of their own institutions or businesses. The three drivers discussed above are not unique to New Zealand. But the New Zealand lesson has been that they are the necessary conditions for effective reform.

NOTES

The observations and views expressed in this paper are those of the author and do not necessarily reflect the official position or policies of the New Zealand Defence Force.

1. It would be misleading to specify results in more detailed terms because systems for reporting financial performance have been evolving over the last five years and there is only a general basis for five-year to five-year period comparisons.

REFERENCES

Handy, C. (1995), *The Empty Raincoat: Making Sense of the Future*, London: Arrow Books.

Kennedy, J.F. (1964), *Profiles in Courage*, New York: Harper & Row Publishers, memorial edition.

New Zealand, State Services Commission (1996), *New Zealand's State Sector Reform: A Decade of Change*, Wellington, NZ: State Services Commission.

Prebble, R. (1996), *I've Been Doing Some Thinking*, Auckland, NZ: Seaview Publishing.

Roth, D. (1993), *Sacred Honor: A Biography of Colin Powell,* San Francisco, CA: Harper San Francisco.

Schick, A. (1996), *The Spirit of Reform: Managing the New Zealand State Sector in a Time of Change*, Wellington, NZ: State Services Commission and the Treasury.

CHAPTER THREE

Managing Defence in the Post-Cold War Era: A View from the United Kingdom

Martin Edmonds

> But it is from within the organisation that the greatest threat comes. We now have MBA managers so preoccupied with systems, recording and checking, that they have stopped valuing their most precious resource, their staff. A refreshing management thinker, Henry Mintzberg, has described MBA courses as attracting neither creative nor generous people and eventually producing the trivial strategist rather than the visionary who empowers workers.
>
> Joyce Bland, The Independent 23 April 1997

MANAGERIALISM RAMPANT

Management is, perhaps, one of the more dominant features of western society in the latter half of this century. It has, arguably, become an integral, if not central, aspect of western culture. It is characterized by the high value that is apparently placed on degrees and qualifications — many of which used to be a help in securing top jobs in commerce and industry and now are a prerequisite, awarded by schools of management or business in universities. The Harvard Masters of Business Administration (MBA) epitomizes this development. How executives managed before this "scientific" focus on management is a matter for conjecture. Perhaps they did not; it was merely that life before the end of the Second World War was slower and less complicated, profits were smaller, losses not so catastrophic and the market generally less cut-throat or uncompromising.

The emergence of the all-influential manager was a phenomenon that drew Burnham to recognize, as early as 1942, that power had inexorably shifted from those who owned wealth and capital to those who "managed" it on their behalf. A new class was emerging in western capitalist society — what Galbraith referred to as the new "technostructure" — who took decisions directed at optimizing return on capital for those who had invested in commercial and industrial enterprise. As corporations grew in size and the scale of their operations expanded, often spreading beyond national boundaries, the notion of "ownership" of capital became less relevant. If there was ownership, it was in the name of "collective" ownership that in its turn was "managed" by large financial institutions, such as insurance societies and pension funds.

Thus, in parallel with state-owned enterprises in which, in theory at least, the population at large had a collective stake, there were organizations and institutions managing on behalf of their clients sums of money paid in small premiums over long periods of time that were invested in commerce and business. Concepts of money management, portfolio management, business management, resource management, finance management, account management — the list is endless — became part of the lexicon of the business world. But this was the business world, the world of the free market, of profit and loss, success or failure. There were those who thought that concepts of management could not become so contagious that they would infect the worlds of government, and the professions where precepts of leadership, service, command, authority, and sacrifice held sway.

They were to be proved wrong. Concepts and practices of management have indeed swept, rampant and virtually unstoppable, into the worlds of government and the professions, and specifically into those of security, defence, and the armed forces over the past 30 years at an accelerating pace. In the defence world this started in the United States but to a considerable extent has been overtaken by the United Kingdom in the past 20 years. It is important to identify the drivers behind this sea change since they help point the way to understanding managerial developments since the end of the Cold War.

BACKGROUND TO THE DEFENCE *MANAGERIAL REVOLUTION*: FIRST STEPS

The defence world lagged significantly behind the world of business and commerce in embracing managerial principles and practices for the simple reason that the idea of national security was so paramount, both in the face of fascism and then postwar communism, that the first priority was vigilance, containment, and escalation dominance. Driven by the sobering lessons of failure to stop the Second World War and a widespread fear of a third world war, national resources on both sides of the Atlantic were appropriated to meet and keep ahead in what was seen as an "arms race" with the Soviet bloc.

The first glimmer of suspicion that perhaps something was wrong started in the United States during the mid-1950s where doubt was cast on the effects that high levels of defence spending were having on American democracy itself. This manifested itself in two forms: first, there was anxiety that possibly the US armed services had entered into some form of conspiracy with branches of the federal government and defence manufacturers, from which the notion of a "military-industrial complex" emerged; and, second, to many the level of public accountability for that spending was alarmingly low and the institutions of government were not equipped to do much about it.

The first anxiety spawned numerous critiques of what was happening in the United States in the late 1950s, foremost among which was *Power Elite*, by C. Wright Mills which cogently argued that power in the United States had become concentrated among a small number of individuals within government, the military, and industry. Such was the strength of his argument that Eisenhower himself warned of what had happened in his farewell address, calling upon Americans to be aware and vigilant so as to slow down or arrest the trend.

The concern for its implications was such that Sam Huntingdon and Morris Janowitz felt compelled to ask the question whether the American military might not usurp government in the name of national security. Both concluded, with varying degrees of conviction, that this could not happen largely for reasons of "professionalism." But out of Janowitz's analysis one pointer to future developments emerged: he referred to the armed services' function as the "constrained management of violence." In that one passing observation, which meant something very different to what it means today, a new complexion on the armed services and defence had been cast.

The second was to have a more profound and lasting effect. US defence spending at the time was seemingly running out of control and increasing year by year. All three services were demanding, and justifying, budget increases to meet what was perceived as an implacable and hostile opponent. The Kennedy administration came to power on a defence policy designed to strengthen American defence. This might normally have been interpreted as a mandate to increase defence spending, but the incoming administration saw it as a commitment to strengthen defence through the more efficient use of existing, or lower, resource levels. Defence was to be seen in future as a commodity, no different from any other good or service purchased by the federal government. As a consequence, defence and security were subject to economic analysis as any other aspect of the market or the economy. The revolution that this seemingly radical initiative introduced is still in evidence today.

The objective of "efficiency" in defence, especially in matters of weapon systems research, development, and procurement, was to achieve national defence capability at less cost to the American taxpayer. There was no simple methodology for doing this in the early 1960s without radically changing the way that defence decisions were made and the different and many out-turns of the defence effort identified and costed against the defence roles and functions they were designed to achieve. Under the direction of Secretary of Defense Robert MacNamara, a group of economists was brought in to look at the way the Pentagon went about its business and to introduce radical change designed to improve decisionmaking effectiveness, give visibility, promote accountability, and achieve overall efficiency. Their approach was to look at defence as nothing more or less than a service and, as such, it was no different from any other good or service to which the laws of economics applied.

Doubtless the sorts of changes that were incorporated into defence decisionmaking in the early 1960s would have been introduced sooner or later. The important point, however, is not when they were introduced, but the effect that they were to have on how defence policy planning and implementation would be viewed in the future. Unlike the past system, in which each of the armed services planned to be able to provide a capability that was at the service of the nation separately or jointly within a Treasury-defined budget ceiling (Snyder 1964, p. 201), the new approach defined what the defence objectives were and sought appropriate ways of achieving them in the most cost-effective way. The new approach, Planning, Programming, and Budgeting System (PPBS), effectively opened the door for the later introduction of management principles and practices, the objective of which was continually to promote efficiency and value-for-money.

The United Kingdom made a gesture toward adopting the PPBS practice soon after the US with the Ministry of Defence (MoD) taking the lead. However, whilst paying lip service to PPBS, its implementation was half-hearted at best and obstructed at worst. The impact was therefore not as dramatic as its proponents anticipated mainly because it was "not in anyone's interests. Analysts upset the natural order of 'departmental decision-making'"(Miller 1990, p. 143). Furthermore, it took the MoD time to introduce the necessary structural changes and during that period Britain, like many other European states, had moved into a "corporatist" phase primarily under a Labour administration. It was a period when Keynesian economic principles still found favour and the security priority remained a robust defence posture in the face of what were perceived to be overwhelming Soviet forces arraigned against Western Europe. The contribution that PPBS made, in general terms, was to shift the focus of defence decisionmaking toward the out-turn, rather than service inputs, and to improve the information available to Parliament and the general public.

PPBS — for all its faults, and with its introduction into the MoD there were many — was a prerequisite for what was to follow by way of a "managerial revolution" in defence. There had to be a realization and an acceptance that defence was not of such paramount concern that it was exempt from or above matters of resource management, cost-efficiency, limited budgets, and accountability. The argument that military affairs and national security were matters for professionals, to be dealt with in secret and not to be short-changed because of the effect this would have on morale, recruitment, operational effectiveness, and commitment, carried weight during times of international crisis and tension; they were less convincing with international détente and shifting national priorities. For the old ways to be swept aside and new approaches to be adopted, there would have to be some national trauma, domestic crisis, or social collapse. In the UK, this came, somewhat unexpectedly, with the domestic financial crises of 1978-79.

DRIVERS BEHIND THE INTRODUCTION OF MANAGERIALISM IN THE MoD

Change within any society or its institutions of government do not happen overnight, or even over a short period; it is more an evolutionary, or gradual process. This essentially is what happened as managerialism became part of the ethos and way of doing business in the United Kingdom and in the MoD throughout the 1980s and early 1990s. In a manner of speaking, this was one facet of what has been labelled the "Thatcher Revolution," or the "Thatcher Years." Within the MoD, however, there were several drivers behind the introduction, and then the enlargement of managerialism — each building on the previous one.

These drivers originated principally from the Conservative government's views on the proper relationship between government as being responsible for policy on the one hand and the providers of goods and services on the other. Though its contents remain classified, the essence of the government's approach to Whitehall were encapsulated in a Cabinet Paper dated April 1980 by Sir Derek Rayner entitled *The Conventions of Government*. The paper was, in effect, his charter for the better management of the state. "Its cumulative impact was considerable and, in so far as these things are knowable, permanent" (Hennessy 1991, p. 470).

It was not the role of government, Thatcher's government argued, to be both policymakers and providers. The target was to reduce the role of government to that of deciding and defining policy and where possible contract out to the private sector the provision of public services. This view applied across the whole spectrum of public services from the public utilities via social welfare to defence. In the process it was believed that three benefits would accrue: the burgeoning size of the civil service would be substantially reduced; the provision of public services would be subject to open competition; and there would be a significant increase in efficiency. The critical consideration would be to ensure that there was adequate oversight of these contracted-out services to ensure maximum public accountability.

Perhaps the most significant by-product of this new approach to the responsibility and role of government was that it freed ministers and civil servants from the day-to-day details of providing public services, leaving them to focus on the more important matters of defining policy and setting strategic goals. But it also had a further by-product which raises fundamental questions about the role and function of government. By hiving off more and more responsibility to the private sector, government departments would also be passing the risk to their contractors. Not only would private corporations be taking the financial risk for the contracts they received, but they would also over time put themselves in a stronger position and effectively establish themselves as private monopoly suppliers.

To understand fully the development of post-Cold War defence management from a UK perspective, it is helpful first to track the overall approach of successive Thatcher governments between 1979 and 1990, since they set the foundation upon which Prime Minister John Major and his defence secretaries carried defence management concepts a stage further. Essentially, John Major's government accepted all that had gone before and were responsive to the same drivers that had featured under Thatcher. The only thing that was different was the changed international security environment and domestic pressure to see a post-Cold War "peace dividend" manifested in the determination of government spending priorities.

The Collapse of Corporatism

As the 1970s drew to a close, it became manifestly clear that neither Britain nor Britain's defences could continue as they had throughout the 1960s and 1970s. Inflation had reached hitherto unknown levels, interest rates were high, national output was declining, and unemployment was rising. The 1978 "Winter of Discontent" proved to be the culmination point of crisis and collapse. Although the Labour government had recognized by 1977 what needed to be done, it had been forced by the International Monetary Fund (IMF), as a condition of a substantial loan, to take remedial action to bring down public spending and reduce public borrowing. Keynesian economics did not work; states could not spend their way out of an economic or social crisis. Into this situation Margaret Thatcher's new government was elected with a new economic approach — monetarism — to take firm but decisive decisions to bring the British economy under control.

Ideology

The term ideology might not be strictly correct when labelling the Thatcher government's style and focus of government, but the principles of monetarism, free-market competition, and non-intervention by government certainly had the mantle of ideology and guided policy decisions in all spheres of government, including defence. It was a matter almost of faith that persuaded Thatcher and her ministers that it was not the government's business to run industry or public services since this was a monopolistic practice and therefore non-competitive. Where monopolies existed there was no incentive to be efficient, and this was at the heart of Britain's industrial and commercial decline. Throughout the 1980s and early 1990s, the Conservative administration embarked on a wholesale policy of privatizing nationalized industries and utilities, selling off public assets and promoting competition. The effects over time were to reduce the size of the public sector and bring down the level of public sector borrowing. The MoD and the armed services were not exempt from this "privatization" ideology.

Reducing the Level of Public Spending

It was apparent to most that the main contributory cause of the economic crisis of the late 1970s was the high level of public spending. It was also felt that the existing levels of taxation were virtually at their maximum, and further tax increases would have two effects: to stultify individual and corporate initiative and to precipitate a backlash from the public at large. To continue to borrow on the international money market or, worse still, to print money would merely fuel an already high level of inflation. Public spending had to be brought down whilst, at the same time, endeavours had to be made to honour public sector commitments in education, health, welfare, pensions, and, inevitably, defence.

At the time that Margaret Thatcher came to power, the objective of reduced public spending meant that all major spending departments of state had to be immediately examined for areas where cuts could be made. It was not the most auspicious time to look at defence — a department that annually spent approximately 12.4 percent of total government spending — for significant cuts. For a start, not only had she been elected on a mandate to redress the serious in-service pay and salaries, resulting from the previous government's policies, as well as strengthen Britain's defence posture that had been allowed to decline during the years of supposed détente, but she also had to take a major spending decision on the future of the British nuclear deterrent — a decision that had been deferred for almost two years (Dillon 1988, pp. 29-30).

The drive to reduce public spending did not abate, and having dispensed with the services of her first secretary of state for defence, Francis Pym, she charged his successor, John Nott, with the task of reviewing defence with the specific purpose of achieving an overall reduction in total defence expenditure. The Nott recommendations targeted the Royal Navy, and in particular its amphibious capabilities and surface vessels, for deep reductions whilst transferring most of their anti-submarine warfare functions to submarines.

The Argentinean invasion of the Falklands Islands and South Georgia and the subsequent war in 1982 effectively brought to an end the intentions of the Nott Defence Review (UK, MoD 1981). Instead of reducing the Navy's surface fleet, it was increased and new carrier task forces were created. This increase, along with strengthening the other two services, was in line with honouring an undertaking made to NATO allies to increase defence spending in real terms at a rate of 5 percent for five years in the face of seriously deteriorating relations with the Soviet Union.

In other words, the driver behind improved defence management has come more out of an apparent inability to reduce Britain's defence commitments than to reduce levels of public spending. This was the case in 1981 and later in 1991 during a further defence review in the wake of the collapse of the Warsaw Pact and the breakup of the Soviet Union. If Britain's defence policy and strategy could not be altered or commitments substantially reduced, then ways for financial savings would have to be found to achieve the same objectives either with fewer resources or with the same resources more efficiently managed and operated.

The Drive for Efficiency

As Britain moved into the 1980s, it was evident that it was not merely a matter of the UK dropping significantly in the international league table of per capita income but also that British goods and services were less and less competitive on the international market. Numerous companies that had been almost household names after the Second World War had disappeared whilst the states of the Pacific Rim were becoming unassailable in those markets where British companies had once been significant players. It was, therefore, not simply a matter of the government creating the conditions for competition and for private industry to be released from government intervention, but to promote where possible, efficiency in both the private and the public sectors. Here, again, the MoD was not exempt.

Efficiency in government became something of a byword. The drive for efficiency was both the attempt to remove old and wasteful practices in the civil service and armed forces that had changed little over the years and had brought a certain degree of contempt from the public and the private sector as well as an expression of the conviction that management practices from the commercial and manufacturing worlds could and should be introduced into government and the public sector. Nowhere was this better exemplified than in the government's appointment of an efficiency in government "supremo," Sir Derek Rayner, in 1979 to start up an Efficiency Unit within the Cabinet Office. This unit was charged with the task of auditing each government department — Rayner's Raiders — with the intention of identifying where new practices could be introduced and money-saving efficiencies achieved (Smith 1996, p. 6; Hennessy 1991, pp. 470-71).

The response of the Ministry of Defence to such intrusion into their internal practices was to establish a top-level directorate general of management and budget charged with the responsibility of streamlining its internal organization. The task of the directorate was to emphasize departmental efficiency and to respond to the government's 1982 Financial Management Initiative (FMI) that called for all government departments to formulate detailed plans for effecting greater efficiency (Cooper 1987, pp. 112-15). A first response was to introduce a system of Responsibility Budgets (RBs). This gave line managers a degree of autonomy over their budgets in a system of devolved authority that was in line with the recommendations of the 1982 Reeves report on financial accountability.

In anticipation of what was to come, the then permanent under-secretary of defence, Sir Frank Cooper, initiated an examination and assessment of a practice that had been introduced in the Department of Environment called the Management Information System for Ministers and Top Management (MINIS). When Michael Heseltine replaced John Nott at the MoD from Environment in 1982 he arrived to find that the MoD were already familiar with the system as well as its parallel system of Cost-Centre Accounting and Budget System for Administrative Expenditure (MAXIS).

Within two years both had been incorporated, along with RBs, within the department. In introducing them, Heseltine had changed the management culture within the department and challenged and altered past assumptions about the "central responsibility for financial planning and control of the defence program that had prevailed over the previous two decades" of functional costings (Smith 1996, p. 7). Through Michael Heseltine, the groundwork was being laid which, from the MoD's perspective, would lead to the managerial changes and practices that have characterized the department's post-Cold War development. These were: the definition of individual responsibility; enhanced delegation of authority for specific defence functions; greater accountability; and a commitment to contracturization (ibid.). Heseltine had introduced within the MoD a "new orthodoxy," one that placed an emphasis on controlling the defence budget through managerial change and personnel cuts (Secretary of State for Defence 1984). Where it was less successful was in managing to monitor and control equipment programs.

Accountability

The major claim by the protagonists of PPBS was that it enabled both ministers and Parliament to have a clearer picture of where public money was being spent and what the longer term implications were of annual expenditures, especially on costly equipment programs, that lasted in excess of ten years. Pre-PPBS, or functional program budgeting, gave detailed figures of spending categories such as training, operations, equipment, salaries, etc. but there was no way of relating these to specific defence policy objectives. Certainly this changed somewhat after 1966, but the exercise of central financial control over program expenditures was cumbersome, bureaucratic, and more often than not incorrect, late or unclear.

The problem also lay in the relevant data being held by the services or within the MoD, but seldom collated in a form that was of use to ministers. The newly established Defence Committee of the House of Commons often registered its frustration with its inability to get a clear picture of defence expenditure to establish whether or not there was waste or room for improvement. It was a charge levelled at the MoD also by the Public Accounts Committee and the National Audit Office (NAO).

It is perhaps worthwhile reflecting briefly on the role of the National Audit Office over this period of change. In the 1960s, the role of the comptroller and auditor general was to audit the financial books of the government departments to ensure that there was fiscal propriety and that monies appropriated were spent in accordance with the estimates presented to and agreed by Parliament. The audited books and the comptroller's report on government expenditure would be submitted to the Commons' Public Accounts Committee and areas where it was thought that departments might be questioned were highlighted. On becoming the NAO, its role has significantly changed: the focus is less on the audit of government accounts and more on the management and efficiency of government departments. While not acting precisely as management consultants, it has been the practice of the NAO to pick out certain activities of government departments, analyze them, and recommend ways that the management and implementation of those activities might be improved and made more cost-effective.

In other words, the management of public resources, primarily taxpayers' money, has become a priority of government departments and agencies, those hybrid organizations that are within the public sector but tasked with operating as if they were private companies with a requirement to cover their operating costs, if not make a profit. Such agencies are accountable to their sponsoring departments and through them to Parliament. Since they, as agencies, are responsible for the delivery of a service but not for policies, the focus of their accountability is their efficiency and competitiveness, not the policy objectives they are charged with achieving.

The Distribution of Risk

It was Margaret Thatcher's contention that the government had overall responsibility for setting policy goals and steering the ship of state. It was at risk only inasmuch as the electorate disagreed with those objectives or if the government failed to deliver on promises. As far as the delivery of public services was concerned, she had faith that the forces of a free market would not merely promote efficiency but also help establish the best means by which they could be delivered. If these were in the public sector, there would be no incentive to seek new methods or to be efficient. Government guarantees and subsidies, while they might still ensure that the goods and services were delivered, were not subject to any sanctions outside the disciplines of the civil service. It was not so much a question of the integrity of civil servants but one of the processes under which they worked, processes that Derek Rayner found on investigation to be antiquated, time-consuming, heavily bureaucratic, and for the most part, redundant.

The target was to put pressure on the providers of public goods and services. This meant subjecting them to the penalties inherent in inefficiency in a competitive free market. Furthermore, it meant that these providers had to be subject to an element of risk, inasmuch as there had to be penalties and sanctions associated with failure or inefficiency. Nowhere was this more evident than within the Ministry of Defence. Whilst the Heseltine reforms applied specifically to information gathering, decisionmaking and resource allocation within the ministry itself, they did not initially apply to the issue of the procurement of defence weapons and equipment. The tasks of making defence procurement more efficient and to introduce change fell to Sir Peter Levene, an industrialist.

The problem over military equipment and weapons procurement was that costs were rising inexorably and exponentially each year. Major acquisition program cost estimates were escalating out of control, and delivery dates were being exceeded — sometimes in excess of two or three times contractual undertakings. The core of the problem was seen as the lack of competition in the weapons market and the public ownership of the major defence manufacturers. There was, in effect, no incentive for efficiency, and defence manufacturers were seen as being "cushioned" and left to do what they wanted more or less at their own pace. Following a series of state defence manufacturing privatization, which saw British Shipbuilder, the British Aircraft Corporation, and the Royal Ordnance factories go to the private sector, Levene introduced radical changes to the weapons procurement process itself by creating and then stimulating competition, and by shifting the responsibility for the management and conduct of defence contracts onto the manufacturer through a system of fixed price contracts.

The system essentially was one of taking away from the MoD and the services' procurement officers the responsibility for defining and specifying in minute detail the content and specification of all new weapons systems. In its place, the MoD Procurement Executive introduced a procurement system that set the "cardinal points" for future weapons systems that defence manufacturers would be required to meet. The details of how these cardinal points would be met was the responsibility of the contractors, and in bidding for the contract they would be free to come up with their own solutions. To a degree this initiative coincided with technological developments that in their turn contributed to the revolution in defence equipment, for example, this was the rapid development in information technology and microelectronics in the civilian sector that had overtaken and in some areas overshadowed defence technologies. The concept of "dual-use technology" became recognized and with it the need to specify components only to military standards was more or less eliminated; indeed, civilian standards often exceeded those of defence.

When it is recognized that modern weapons are increasingly dependent upon electronic subsystems and that components of these subsystems are also available on the civilian market, the distinction between a defence and a civilian manufacturer becomes increasingly blurred. This increasing overlap between the two sectors was to give a boost to the objective of promoting competition within the defence market, for it became increasingly feasible for major companies that were not traditionally defence manufacturers to consider competing for prime defence contracts. Furthermore, as weapons systems became more complex and their composition driven increasingly by computers and software, the assumption that only the platform manufacturer was competent enough to design, manufacture, integrate and assemble modern weapons — and therefore was the only realistic prime contractor — became less convincing.

Correspondingly, competition for prime defence contracts, against early expectations, have become more, not less, possible with companies with system design and integration skills or with a good record of managing complex civil programs entering the defence market. Whichever company becomes a prime contractor, however, it is now accepted that it has to carry the risk not only for delivering the product to agreed specification and performance but also for any financial losses incurred.

POST-COLD WAR DEVELOPMENTS: MoD'S NEW MANAGEMENT STRATEGY

With an annual budget in the region of £23 billion (1990 prices) or 4.2 percent of GNP during the late 1980s, defence was an obvious and potentially available target for the government's policy of reducing public spending. In fact, the demands of the Cold War and the inescapable commitments in Northern Ireland and to home defence made it difficult to reduce spending on forces that were known to be overstretched. On the contrary, the introduction of cost-saving measures and improved efficiency within the MoD and the armed services was aimed more at making it easier to meet defence policy roles and tasks within the defence budget ceiling rather than redistributing money saved to the civilian sector or to reducing public sector borrowing. The end of the Cold War and the collapse of the Warsaw Pact effectively removed the rationale for maintaining high levels of defence spending, and cuts in the defence budget were to become a prime government target.

Lest it was thought that the Thatcher revolution in the style and conduct of government and Whitehall management had run its course, and that further changes to the manner in which the MoD and other government departments conducted their business was unnecessary, the recommendations of Sir Robin Ibbs, Sir Derek Rayner's replacement as the Cabinet Office's Efficiency Unit, shattered any illusions. Mrs Thatcher still saw scope for further reductions in both the central control and the overmanning of Whitehall departments. In 1987, prior to the general election, Sir Robin Ibbs filed a report entitled *The Next Steps* in which he recommended a restructuring of the civil service into a small core of policymakers with the remainder engaged only in providing goods and services as free standing agencies, operating as small businesses, and regulated by independent authorities. These recommendations struck at the very heart of a civil service that had exercised central control over every item of public expenditure since the end of the First World War (Hennessy 1991, p. 471; 1990). No department of state was exempt from its recommendations, not least the MoD.

One consequence for the MoD of the Ibbs *Next Steps* recommendations was a requirement to achieve cumulative improvement in efficiency averaging 2.5 percent each year for three years starting in April 1993. The efficiency program covered about two-thirds of the defence budget which, in monetary terms, translated into target input savings of £1 billion. The department, in fact, exceeded the target of £2.1 billion only to be required to meet a further efficiency target of 1.5 percent over the following four years to 1995 (UK, MoD 1991c, p. 53). To enable the MoD to achieve these demanding targets when no significant change to defence policy objectives had yet been made other than a shift in priorities from Europe and the defence of the Eastern Atlantic to home defence, out-of-area operations, and a commitment to rapid reaction forces within Europe, the department planned a further management change under the title of the New Management Strategy (NMS).

According to the MoD, the NMS was a system of management planning that would allow the department to focus on the defence output more effectively. It built on the MINIS system and RBs; eliminated the parallel system of RBs and centralized control that prevailed in the 1980s; and allowed budget-holders to prepare a plan each year in parallel with their bid for resources. In this way, they would define the output they undertook to deliver with the resources (funds) allocated to them. When it was finally incorporated into the MoD in April 1993, this devolved system of management formally brought to an end the centralized system of financial control within the MoD by allowing service commanders and managers to run their activities within a single budget under their control. The argument behind the change was that resources could be linked more directly to out-turn; out-turn could be weighed against objectives; performance could be measured; and greater flexibility within budgets could be achieved as rigid, centrally determined spending categories no longer applied and could be discarded (ibid., pp. 60-61).

The output for which the 21 Top Level Budget-Holders (TLBs) would be responsible was guided by a MoD "Departmental Plan." Before any spending could go ahead, the plan had to be agreed to by the Financial Planning and Management Group (FPMG) which defined the objectives that were sought by the MoD and set them alongside the resources available for defence. The plan was also to be set within the framework of the Long-Term Costings (LTC) exercise that projected future costs over a ten-year period against spending commitments (ibid., p. 55; UK, MoD 1989, pp. 18-19). Responsibility for ensuring that decisions in respect of the Departmental Plan were affordable and that they achieved the best value for money rested with the second permanent under-secretary of defence who chaired an Office of Management and Budget (OMB) and was assisted by a Resources and Programmes Staff (RP).

In order that Whitehall departmental spending priorities and plans were in line with the government's overall spending plans, after 1991 each was required to prepare a report to explain its objectives, describe its planned expenditure, and highlight key areas of performance. These reports replaced individual chapters in the Public Expenditure White Paper and, in the case of the MoD, provided a more detailed and accurate account of its Departmental Plan, objectives, resources, and management performance than the annual Statement on the Defence Estimates (UK, MoD 1992*a*, p. 1).

The MoD's Departmental Plan not only defined objectives — currently there are nine — but also laid down the management priorities of the department. These could reflect government-wide initiatives, such as Sir Robin Ibbs's *Next Steps*, or matters of particular concern to defence. Among the stated departmental objectives, however, in addition to clearly stated military tasks, was the commitment to "Good Practice and Departmental Standards" (Objective 8) and "Efficiency and Effectiveness" (Objective 9). The concept of accountability was also carried forward by which all management areas and budget-holders were formally held accountable for their performance through a comprehensive review of their activity.

POST-COLD WAR DEVELOPMENTS: NEXT STEPS, 1992

It should be evident that, through the NMS, responsibility for finding savings and promoting efficiency within defence, but not at the expense of achieving declared aims and objectives, was delegated to the TLBs or, more specifically, the senior military and defence civilian personnel. In a manner of speaking, this was a shrewd political move, since the services had become the gamekeeper, having been identified as the poacher over the years. Furthermore, because of their close knowledge and experience of the areas for which they now had management and financial responsibility, they were expected to be able to identify areas of significant saving. Initially this proved to be the case and some significant savings through altered practices were found. The outcome of this achievement was that the government, seeking further cuts in public expenditure at the time, revised the efficiency "target" of the Ministry of Defence up from 1.5 percent per annum in 1991-92 to 2.5 percent for the following two years. The effect on morale and service personnel opinions of the priorities of the TLBs was soon evident.

The thrust of the Ibbs report, however, was taken up by the government, and the MoD, along with other departments, was required to look to areas where the provision of goods and services could be handed over to the private sector or to quasi-autonomous "agencies." Expressed in terms of it making "a substantial contribution to the government's Next Steps Initiative," the MoD in 1992 took its first step to set up agencies that hitherto had come within its own organizational structure. Eleven agencies were created that year involving 28,000 civilians and 8,000 service personnel with a combined annual turnover of £1.7 billion. Seven operated within the defence chain of command and were redesignated Defence Support Agencies (DSA). The most significant of these was the new Defence Research Agency (DRA). As an executive agency of the MoD, it assumed the functions of four former defence research establishments (UK, MOD 1991*b*, p. 7).

The Ibbs report was not the only central government initiative that would have implications for the MoD at this time: in November 1991, the government issued a White Paper *Competing for Quality* which set out proposals for extending competition in the provision of services in the public sector (UK, HMG 1991). In response, the MoD started letting-out contracts for services in areas such as logistics, headquarters, operational commands, and agencies hitherto performed in-house. It was a practice that the department was committed to widen in subsequent years(UK, MoD 1992*b*, p. 50). The manner in which this was pursued was to expose in-house services to private sector competition and market testing. The first year of operation resulted in 21 contracts being issued at a net saving to the defence budget of £5.7 million per year (UK, MoD 1992*a*, p. 21).

Since its introduction in 1991, the MoD's *Next Steps* agencies have increased in number as more and more services are contracted-out to the private sector or the free-standing defence agencies operating through a trading fund. In 1992, five further agencies were added to DRA and the Meteorological and Hydrographic Offices involving a further 19,000 service and civilian personnel. By mid-1992, "taken together, the Agencies now operating account for some £1,700 million, or 32 percent of MoD annual running costs, and employ around 3,500 personnel" (ibid., p. 18).

From 1992 onwards, the MoD steadily developed both its New Management Strategy and *Next Steps* launch of Defence Support Agencies (DSA). In 1993 four more DSAs were created bringing the total since the scheme was introduced to 14 covering some 37,000 military and civilian staff (UK, MoD 1993, p. 21). The following year, 1994, the number increased to 16, affecting a total of 38,000 personnel (UK, MoD 1994*a*, p. 29), and the year after to 21 involving 44,000 people (UK, MoD 1995*a*, p. 26). By March 1995, the MoD was in a position to make the assertion that a large proportion of the MoD's work is now carried out by agencies. These bodies operate within a policy and resource framework which encourages a business-like approach to the delivery of services to the MoD and, where appropriate, to the public (ibid. Annex C, p. xi).

Among the agencies were those responsible for logistic information; RAF signals engineering; RAF training; naval aircraft repair for helicopters of all three services; maintenance group defence for storage and distribution of aerosystems parts, engineering and electronic communications services; defence operational analysis; defence accounts; and army base repair; in addition to defence research; postal services; and animal training and veterinary support services. There is little evidence that the exercise of creating defence agencies has run its course. The claims of significant cost savings as a consequence of putting them on a "business-like" footing and encouraging them to be more commercial in their approach would appear to be incentive enough to find more opportunities. These agencies have, meanwhile, also been following the guidelines laid down in the MoD's Competing for Quality initiative (UK, MoD 1995*b*, p. 94). So also has the MoD assiduously prosecuted its policy of market testing for the provision of goods and services that are not liable for agency status but which could be provided by private commercial organizations and businesses. In some instances these services can be engaged by the MoD itself and, in others, as a consequence of initiatives taken by top, middle and low level budget-holders in their respective pursuit of increased cost-effectiveness in the execution of their responsibilities.

By 1993, the overall perspective of defence management within the MoD and its place within its *Departmental Defence Aims and Objectives* was more or less in place. Within the framework of overall government policy, two broad areas of policy could be identified: defence policy and management policy. These in turn could be expressed in terms of three interrelated department aims. The first aim referred to the formulation of defence policy and the construction of a defence program — or programs — to give it effect. These were expressed in terms of defence roles, military tasks, force structures and levels, readiness and equipment programs. Together, these shaped defence capability.

The third departmental aim was that of "good management." Essentially this was the commitment to ensure efficient management throughout the MoD and the armed services and was to be manifest in a departmental efficiency program, market testing, restructuring, rationalization and *Next Step* defence support agencies. In order to manage the MoD efficiently, two elements were identified which provided a guideline. The first was efficiency, defined within any year as the delivery of required outputs as efficiently as possible within allocated resources and in compliance with MoD policies and standards and to plan for continuous improvements in efficiency in the future. The second addressed department standards, particularly in respect of meeting constitutional, legal, and government requirements, to be a "good and fair employer promoting the morale, motivation, and welfare of military and civilian personnel" (ibid., p. 4).

The degree to which this departmental aim achieved its objectives would bear directly on improving defence capability. Defence capability, the department's second aim, corresponded to the output of defence and amounted to overall UK military capability as reflected in four principal capabilities. The first was the provision of military capability, namely of forces of the required size, capability, and readiness that would meet the military tasks indicated by government defence policy and funded in the defence program. The second was the provision of equipment capability by the management of the defence equipment program to meet planned levels in the future supported by a program of technology demonstration and research. The third capability was that of an operational headquarters with the required capability to undertake contingency planning for, and the higher direction of, agreed military tasks. The last capability objective was that of headquarters support services necessary to manage and deploy the armed forces (ibid., p. 5).

MANAGEMENT AND THE COMMERCIALIZATION OF DEFENCE

The initiatives introduced into government in general and the MoD in particular by the Thatcher government and subsequently by the Major administration might have reached their apogee by 1994 since, by then the more obvious defence support agencies had been identified and established and the practice of market testing had become part of the working culture of the new budget-holders within the New Management Strategy system. This did not, however, take into account a sudden and unexpected demand from the Treasury in 1993 to find further savings over and above the force reductions to all three services in 1991 of up to a quarter of all personnel overall that had been introduced in the wake of the defence review *Options for Change* announced in July 1990 (UK, MoD 1991*a*, p. 4; 1991*b* p. 40). In response to this additional burden, the MoD initiated an exercise under the title *The Defence Costs Study* with profound implications for the way in which the MoD and the services would manage their business (UK MoD, 1995*c*).

It might be argued that at the time when the Defence Costs Study was initiated the MoD and the services had become more or less accustomed to their new commercially-oriented practices. In looking to find savings of £750 million within a short space of time without making any reductions to defence policy commitments or to the existing number of defence roles and military tasks, it was perhaps inevitable that the focus fell, first, on any defence functions that could be either hived off to new defence agencies or on the new processes and procedures introduced, such as harnessing the new opportunities offered by information technology. Second, yet more support services could be further put out to competition and market testing.

It is relevant that the exercise was largely undertaken by MoD civilians and service personnel at all levels under a small steering group headed by the secretary of state and an executive group chaired by the minister for procurement. The study looked at the support areas across the board; no area of defence or service activity was exempt. Nothing was to be sacrosanct: tradition, service sacred cows, familiar practices, public sentiment, long established assumptions, and even the separate services themselves — each was held up to scrutiny. Invitations were extended to all branches of the services, and to all levels within the rank structure, to offer novel suggestions to save money. Of particular interest were ideas that crossed service institutional boundaries and examined the "vertical" management structure of each service (UK, MoD 1994*b*, p. 6).

The premise behind the Defence Costs Study was to focus attention specifically on the defence support services and to find ways in which administrative and logistic support could be reduced without any loss of operational effectiveness of fighting capability. Hence the findings of the exercise, when it was published in July 1994, were put under the title *Front Line First*. The study looked at all aspects of defence support and in all 33 individual study teams examined separate areas of business (ibid., pp. 5-9). The outcome was as remarkable as it was, perhaps, unexpected. Not only did the MoD exceed the targets set by the Treasury and within the lead times set down, but additional savings also enabled the MoD to embark on a "substantial programme of investment in new equipment and a range of other important measures designed to sustain and improve operational capability" (UK, MoD 1995*b*, p. 92; 1994*b*, p. 8).

Almost to be expected, one of the areas where the Defence Costs Study identified further savings and improvements in efficiency was in the management structures and procedures of the Ministry of Defence head office and the service headquarters. Noting that the MoD was unique in Whitehall in that it had a dual role as both a department of state and the headquarters of the armed forces as a whole, the separation of the two immediately seemed unnecessary, especially as most of their activities involved both civil and military functions. There were areas of obvious overlap and a tendency for both to operate along vertical lines of authority to the detriment of more cooperative, horizontal practices. One obvious consequence of all this was to integrate the military and civilian staffs "and create a unified structure, provided the structure preserved the clarity of the two roles of policy-making and execution" (UK, MoD 1994*b*, p. 9).

The service headquarters also came under scrutiny and its management practices subject to radical change. Whilst the New Management Strategy had had a significant impact, further scope was found for improvement. The most significant recommendation, much in line with what had been done in the MoD head office, was to break down organizational boundaries between the services. It was deemed prudent to create a permanent joint headquarters in preference to the ad hoc arrangements that had prevailed in response to crises in the past. The joint headquarters at the operational level would be closely linked to the MoD as the policymaking and strategic planning arm. The service chiefs of staff would retain their service identity and functions but work collaboratively. Further rationalization of the service chains of command were envisaged by concentrating staffs in Portsmouth, High Wycombe, and, for the Army, three newly established divisional headquarters in York, Shrewsbury, and Aldershot.

Financial management was also altered, though not in any radical way beyond the reforms introduced under the New Management Strategy. To streamline decisions, Top Level Budget-Holders were not required to provide the MoD head office with financial details as frequently as before, thereby enabling significant reductions to central program staffs. The Front Line First study reaffirmed the principles of delegated budgetary authority but introduced new measures whereby budget-holders and line managers would be held accountable for the resources they received and the results they achieved.

Within personnel areas, the study looked at recruitment, manning, and training. Here again, they found that significant savings were possible, mostly by contracting specific areas out to the private sector and market testing. For example, the function of the services' recruiting offices would be taken over by the Employment Services' Agency as the first point of contact. Manning the services was proving difficult and large numbers of redundant servicemen and women were required to cover for others away from their unit, ship, or workplace. By introducing Local Service Engagements and greater use of reserve or retired personnel, further savings could be achieved with less disruption. Training also was an area for further rationalization, the most radical of which was the decision to dispense with the Service Staff Colleges. In a surge of "jointness'" in line with the service headquarters and MoD head office, a joint services Command and Staff College was established to start functioning in 1997. Other joint training activities introduced included early and basic flight training, helicopter instruction, a defence school of music, and a defence medical service to work in collaboration with the civilian National Health Service.

It was in the areas of equipment procurement and logistic support, the defence estate and support infrastructure that the most significant savings were to be found. Competition was to remain the cornerstone of the procurement executive's philosophy though greater flexibility would be allowed for a single source if the proposals were innovative and cost effective enough to proceed. The MoD's policy of No Acceptable Price, No Contract (NAPNOC) would be strengthened along with new arrangements for contractors to take on more of the risks associated with MoD procurement contracts. Other radical decisions to save on costs were the privatization of service housing and repair facilities, rationalization of storage and spare parts facilities and defence postal services, and the lease of non-specific military vehicles from commercial suppliers.

The impact of the Defence Costs Study on the way the British armed services and MoD go about their business in the future will be profound. It will alter the work culture of the armed services with knock-on implications for the conditions of employment and career structures of those who serve. This was, to some extent, the issue addressed by Sir Michael Bett and his team when engaged to take on an Independent Review of Service Career and Manpower Structures and Conditions of Service. They reported in 1995, making over one hundred recommendations to the way the MoD and the services approached the overall question of personnel management (Bett *et al.* 1995).

The emphasis again was on management, for which the Bett team recommended centralizing responsibility for personnel matters within the MoD and thereby taking it essentially away from each separate service. The merit, or otherwise, of the Bett report's recommendations took almost two years to absorb within the MoD and services; not all recommendations met with approval. Perhaps the most telling criticism of the report, and of the MoD's incorporation of most of its findings, has been that Bett and his colleagues have tended to import human resource practices, career and promotion criteria, and pay scales from civilian organizations without taking adequate account of the nature of service life or the distinctions between peace and war (See Dandeker *et al.* 1997).

MANAGING BRITAIN'S ARMED FORCES IN THE FUTURE

The past 20 years have seen many radical changes to the ways in which the British armed services and MoD have gone about their business. The nature of British defence and security has also changed as the international strategic environment has become less dominated by the assumptions of the Cold War and as the perceived threats to the country have diminished and become less urgent. Correspondingly, the British armed services have declined in number by up to a quarter, the inventory of weapons systems, though in many cases modernized, has been reduced, and the content and focus of defence policy has shifted away from high intensity war to rapid deployment forces in support of operations other than war, peacekeeping, and counterinsurgency at home and abroad. Hand in hand with these reductions has been a steady decline in the size of the defence budget both in absolute and in real terms.

A dominant feature of managerial change has been the extent to which roles and functions, which in the past were assumed by the armed services and performed in-house, have been subjected to market testing and where more "cost-effective" solutions have been contracted out to private suppliers. This has predominantly been in the logistic support area, including research, development, and production of future weapons systems. The Defence Costs Studies of 1994-95 accelerated that process, one that has been extensively conducted throughout all departments of government. The longer term benefits, or costs, of this practice have still to be established. Many feel that as private contractors consolidate their position, the extent to which there is likely to be competition for renewal of their contracts will diminish, leaving private sector monopolies with all the costs to the MoD that such practices imply. There is already some evidence in the area of service catering that this has already started to happen. Furthermore, in times of crisis or emergency, monopoly private suppliers gain further leverage as the shipping companies did during the sealift of materiel during the Gulf War.

A second dominant feature of the managerial changes in the MoD concern the creation of Defence agencies operating within the public sector but as commercial entities operating through a trading fund. The question must arise here of whether the priority of these agencies is to be profitable or to be in support of the nation's defence effort. The latter might well be incompatible with the former, the more so as they are as subject to market testing and competition as private suppliers. The agencies that the MoD has created need, for their continued existence, a regular line of business from the MoD and the services in order to survive. If this is not forthcoming, unlike the more secure arrangements of the past, they might very well go out of business altogether, to the detriment of the overall defence effort.

These two developments, however, are part and parcel of the government's initiatives to reduce the involvement of government in areas that were not thought appropriate. The argument is that governments and ministers are responsible for policies and strategies, not their implementation. The more that the latter can be delegated or contracted out to others, the exercise will be not only more efficient and cost-effective but the risks associated with implementation would also be put onto others. From a defence perspective, the approach threatens to drive a wedge between the political arm of Defence and the executive and further separate the military authorities from the political. Under Margaret Thatcher, the chiefs of staff had effectively been relegated to the equivalent level of assistant undersecretary with planning and advisory responsibilities shared between the civil servants and "purple" — that is to say central defence as opposed to service — military staff. This further extended the schism that had existed from the days when the services lost their separate ministries and ministers of state in the 1960s when they were expected to shoulder all of the responsibilities in war but had none of the decisionmaking power.

Divisions and schisms in the British armed forces have always been around — interservice rivalry, for example, has been a feature of defence life both in respect of operational command and resource allocation. Under the new regime, new divisions have emerged, created by the drive for "value-for-money" budget reductions and all the attendant rhetoric. These include the division between the regular and the reserve forces both in terms of roles and terms of service. There is the division between the "teeth" arms — the front line — and the logistic support, so much of which is in the hands of civilian suppliers. To these must also be added the division between the MoD head office and the services' joint and single service headquarters with split lines of authority. Finally, there is the division between budget-holders with their priorities and those who expect of them ever improved out-turn and efficiency.

The situation that has been created in the wake of New Management Systems, Next Steps, and Front Line First is one in which the armed forces have become distanced from their primary purpose: the need to be ready at short notice to engage with a hostile enemy in the defence of the nation's integrity and interests. The conduct of war is for professionals; the way of war today means that more than the uniformed front-line forces will be in danger. Redundancy is a necessary, not a luxury, in war. In peacetime, decisionmakers can plan and manage affairs at or below the margin. How successful the British armed services will be in future conflicts that require more than 40,000 persons (the number that served in the Gulf War), last longer than ten days, incur significant casualties, and involve numbers of civilians is a critical issue waiting to be addressed.

Perhaps war is less likely and the sorts of forces and force posture that Britain has raised, trained, and paid for in the past are not necessary in the future. The international environment and the new Labour administration's future defence and foreign policy priorities are too uncertain for this to be projected with any degree of certainty. The future of Europe and further collaboration with European partners on bi- and multilateral bases will further complicate the management of defence. The emphasis undoubtedly is on joint national operations and combined operations with Atlantic, European, or UN partners. At the operational level, this emphasis may be achieved; but beyond it there seems to be little or nothing at the margin for which even the best management principles and practices will be sufficient.

REFERENCES

Bett, M. *et al.* (1995), *Independent Review of the Armed Forces' Manpower, Career and Remuneration Structures: Managing People in Tomorrow's Armed Forces*, Report to the Secretary of Defence, London: HMSO.

Cooper, Sir F. (1987), "Ministry of Defence," in *Reshaping Central Government*, ed. J. Harrison and M. Gretton, London: Macmillan.

Dandeker, C., M. Edmonds, J. Higgs and F. Paton (1997), *Bett and Beyond*, Bailrigg Memorandum No. 23, Lancaster, London: CDISS.

Dillon, G.M. (1988), "Britain," in *Defence Policy-Making: A Comparative Analysis*, ed. G.M. Dillon, Leicester, UK: Leicester University Press.

Hennessy, P. (1990), *Whitehall*, London: Fontana.

──── (1991), "Mrs Thatcher's Impact on Whitehall," in *Politics UK*, ed. B. Jones *et al.*, London: Philip Alan.

Miller, D. (1990), "Planning, Programming, Budgeting System and the Case of Rational Decision-making in Britain's Ministry of Defence," *Defense Analysis*, 6 (2):143.

Secretary of State for Defence (1984), *MINIS and the Development of the Organisation of Defence*, London: HMSO.

Smith, A. (1996), *Management of the MoD 1983-1986: The Impact and Legacy of Michael Heseltine*, Bailrigg Memorandum No.15 Lancaster, London: CDISS.

Snyder, W.P. (1964), *The Politics of British Defence Policy 1945-1962*, London: Benn.

United Kingdom, Her Majesty's Government (1991), *Competing for Quality*, Cmnd 1730, London: HMSO.

United Kingdom, Ministry of Defence (1981), *The United Kingdom Defence Programme: The Way Forward*, Cmnd 8299, London: HMSO.

──── (1989), *The Ministry of Defence*, London: MoD Public Relations Service.

──── (1991a), *Britain's Army for the 90s*, Cmnd 1595, London: HMSO.

──── (1991b), *DRA Framework Document, 1991*, London: Ministry of Defence.

_____ (1991c), *Statement on the Defence Estimates, Britain's Defence for the 90s, 1991*, Vol. 1, Cmnd 1559-1, London: HMSO.

_____ (1992a), *The Government's Expenditure Plans 1992/93 to 1994/95: Departmental Report by the Ministry of Defence*, Cmnd 1901, London: HMSO.

_____ (1992b), *Statement on the Defence Estimates*, Cmnd 1981, London: HMSO.

_____ (1993), *Departmental Report by the MoD: The Government's Expenditure Plans 1993/94 to 1995/96*, Cmnd 2201, London: HMSO.

_____ (1994a), *Departmental Report by the MoD: The Government's Expenditure Plans 1994/95 to 1996/97*, Cmnd 2501, London: HMSO.

_____ (1994b), *Front Line First: The Defence Costs Study*, London: Ministry of Defence.

_____ (1995a), *Departmental Report by the MoD: The Government's Expenditure Plans 1995/96 to 1997/98*, London: HMSO.

_____ (1995b), *Statement on the Defence Estimates: Stable Forces in a Strong Britain 1995*, Cmnd 2800, London: HMSO.

CHAPTER FOUR

Distributing the Defence Budget: Choosing Between Capital and Manpower

John M. Treddenick

INTRODUCTION

The 1992 *Statement on Canadian Defence Policy* included the following: "The relative share of the defence budget devoted to capital will increase from 22 percent to 26 percent within four years, while a target figure of 30 percent will be maintained. In contrast, the share devoted to personnel will decrease" (Canada, DND 1992, p. 14).

Two years and a new government later, the 1994 Defence White Paper, more focused on restructuring in the face of policy shifts and portending massive budgetary cuts, was silent on how the budget should be allocated. But the defence estimates which followed in subsequent years clearly reflected the continuing and growing frustrations that the Department of National Defence (DND) was experiencing in finding room for capital expenditures:

> The Department continues its efforts to devote *an increased share* of spending to Capital acquisitions in order to stem the tide of obsolescence and deterioration of essential military equipment in spite of significant reductions to its funding envelope (Canada 1995, p. 26).

> The Department continues its efforts to devote *a minimum essential share* of spending to Capital acquisitions in order to stem the tide of obsolescence of essential military equipment in spite of significant reductions to its funding envelope (Canada 1996, p. 32).

To keep the CF operationally relevant, *a judicious and clearly focused recapitalization* effort will be undertaken, including specific efforts to improve overall strategic mobility and deployability (Canada 1997, pp. 2-9).

This struggle to attain an appropriate and stable balance between funding current operations and funding capital acquisitions has been an enduring theme in the management of Canadian defence policy. Even the unification of the forces in the 1960s, the most drastic restructuring of defence in the postwar period, was inspired, at least in part, by an attempt to redress growing budgetary imbalances (Canada, DND 1964). In more recent years, the end of the Cold War, diminished funding for defence, and an increased tempo of current military operations have made managing this balance particularly difficult.

The balance between current operations and capital acquisitions have critical implications for the operational capabilities of the armed forces, both in the present and in the future. It is no exaggeration, therefore, to suggest that how the budget is allocated is as clear a statement about a country's defence posture as is the size of the budget itself, perhaps even more so. Yet, strangely, there has been no informed debate within the strategic studies community about how Canadian defence budgets are allocated. We have been informed, at least in the past, and apparently confirmed by the 1992 *Statement on Defence* quoted above, that an appropriate allocation for capital would be 30 percent of the defence budget. But this figure has been offered without any evident analytical basis. Even if appropriate at one time, it is surely suspect as an enduring target, given that defence policies change in the face of changing strategic, technical, and economic circumstances. What then is an appropriate distribution? How are we to judge whether 30 or 20 or 40 percent is an appropriate allocation for capital? Are targets of this type really necessary for effective defence budgeting? And if they are, why has DND continued to be frustrated in its attempts to meet them?

This paper is an effort to address these types of questions. It does so first by employing some basic economic ideas in an attempt to clarify the nature of the problem of choosing between capital and manpower. It then examines how the trade-off between them has been handled in the past. Next it attempts to show how current choices and policies with respect to manpower and capital are already shaping future budgetary allocations. This status quo future is contrasted with two alternative futures which are based on modified approaches to structuring the defence budget. These comparisons are then used to draw some inferences about what constitutes an appropriate framework for making choices between capital and manpower.

MAKING DEFENCE ... IN THEORY

To gain some understanding of the defence allocation problem, it is useful to view the making of defence capabilities as a two-stage economic process. In the first stage, governments decide on the level of the defence budget. The state, acting as a rational actor attempting to maximize national economic welfare, is assumed to allocate resources to defence such that the extra security derived from military expenditure is just balanced by its opportunity cost in terms of civilian expenditure foregone. In the second stage, the focus of this paper, defence managers decide on how to spend the defence budget. These managers are assumed to be acting as output-maximizers, in the sense that they allocate the defence budget among manpower, capital, and other defence inputs in such a way as to obtain as much defence capability as possible out of the given budget. It is further assumed that they do so with some concern for the distribution of capabilities over time. In reality, of course, the two stages cannot be independent. Nor can they really be treated simply as economic processes. The outcomes at both levels will emerge from complex political and bureaucratic processes. In these processes interests beyond the efficient allocation of resources will be continuously in play. Nevertheless, viewing the defence choice problem in this way is analytically useful. Even with its obvious oversimplifications, it has the potential to lay clear the underlying economic nature of the defence choice problem.

For purposes of this paper, the problem of determining the level of defence spending will be taken as solved. This simplifies the analysis considerably, if only because defence resource allocation problems at the second stage deal with a well-defined set of resources, with reasonably well-defined objectives, and are managed by a unique decisionmaking agency. Allocation management problems at this stage would at least appear to be more amenable to economic analysis than is the first-stage allocation problem. This is not to minimize the political and bureaucratic pressures which influence how the defence budget is spent. One could easily understand the military, or at least parts of it, having a preference for manpower expenditures. For one thing, manpower levels are often taken as a simple and ready measure of military strength and capability. For another, higher manpower levels increase opportunities for promotion and command. Defence firms, on the other hand, would favour a budgetary distribution biased toward equipment expenditures. They could find allies in politicians and bureaucrats who might favour capital expenditures to achieve industrial and regional economic benefits. There may also be biases in favour of spending on defence support activities such that the political benefits of military spending are distributed in some geographically preferred way.

Despite these potentially powerful influences on the structure of the defence budget, this paper, however naively, takes as its point of departure the assumption that the challenge of defence management is to maximize the defence capability obtainable from the defence budget presented to it. On the basis of this assumption, it is possible to stylize the defence resource allocation problem as an application of the basic microeconomic problem of constrained production. The objective in this problem is to use a fixed budget to acquire that combination of inputs which maximizes output. Given the technological relationship between the output produced and the inputs used, described as a production function, and the relative prices of the inputs, it is possible to solve for that particular combination of inputs which maximizes the output. This optimum combination of inputs determined for a particular budget can be usefully expressed as a ratio of their quantities. Thus, for two inputs — labour and capital — the solution could be expressed as the capital-labour ratio, generally written as the K/L ratio. Given the optimum K/L ratio and the relative prices of capital and labour, the optimal allocation of the fixed budget between capital and labour can then be easily determined.

The analogous problem facing defence managers is shown in schematic form in Figure 1. The output variable is taken to be defence capability. As we shall see, whether that capability can be measured is irrelevant. The three broad aggregates

FIGURE 1: Making Defence

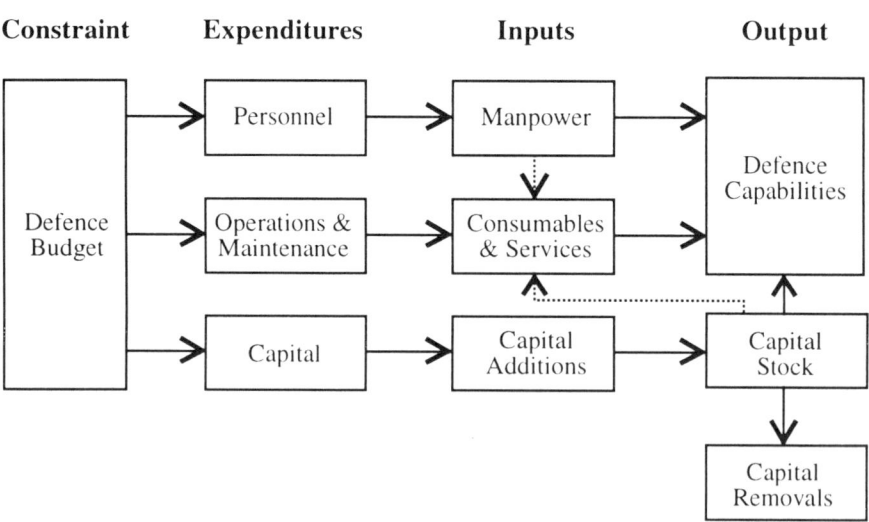

of inputs in the production of defence capability include manpower; capital assets, particularly the quantity and quality of available weapons systems, but also transportation and other support systems; and intermediate inputs or consumables such as ammunition, petrol, food, spare parts, and contract services. However, because the use of intermediate inputs would seem to depend only indirectly on total output and more directly on the level of manpower and capital inputs, it is possible to simplify the analytical problem by reducing the arguments of the defence production function to manpower and capital alone. Thus, the defence production function, if it exists and if it could be discovered, would tell us just what levels of defence capability could be produced for different combinations of manpower and capital. It in effect describes the technologies of making military capability. From the economic point of view, then, the second stage defence management problem becomes one of selecting that combination of manpower and capital which maximizes the defence capability achievable from a given defence budget.[1]

Implicit in the notion of the defence production function is the idea of technical substitution. Over some range, determined by the technology of producing military outputs, capital can supposedly be substituted for labour to produce the same level of military capability. In other words, there exist alternative combinations of manpower and capital which are capable of yielding equal levels of military capability. On the other hand, a given defence budget allows the defence manager the opportunity to select from among many alternative combinations of inputs. The best combination of inputs will be that which maximizes military capability and as before, this combination can be expressed as a particular ratio of capital to manpower. In practical terms, the K/L ratio simply represents a measure of how well, on average, the troops are equipped. High K/L ratios, where the troops are well-equipped, describe capital-intensive methods of producing military capabilities. Lower K/L ratios describe more manpower-intensive methods. Just which K/L ratio maximizes military capabilities for a given budget will depend upon the relative costs of military labour and military capital. Thus, when military manpower costs rise relative to the costs of military capital, we would expect a reallocation of defence budgets away from manpower and toward capital. Alternatively, when equipment costs rise relative to manpower costs, output-maximizing defence managers would seek more manpower-intensive ways of producing defence capability.

The technical process of making defence capabilities has a budgetary equivalent. When intermediate inputs are included, the budgetary expenditures corresponding to the inputs are categorized as personnel expenditures, operations and maintenance expenditures, and capital expenditures. Personnel expenditures include military and civilian pay plus other personnel-related benefits. This expenditure depends directly on the numerical size of the armed forces and on rates of pay and benefits. Operations and maintenance expenditures include expenditures for operating and maintaining facilities and equipment, including engineering services, contracted repair and overhaul, spares, and fuel products for aircraft, ships and vehicles and for such things as travel and transportation. These, like personnel expenditures represent expenditures made to support, either directly or indirectly, the current combat readiness of the military establishment, either in terms of training or in terms of actual operations. They are the payments made for forces-in-being.

Capital expenditures are expenditures made for new equipment and facilities. In a functional sense, capital expenditures differ markedly from personnel expenditures and expenditures for operations and maintenance. They have little, if anything, to do with current combat readiness. Capital expenditures are investments in future capabilities. They are payments for potential forces. Thus, in any given year capital expenditures could be reduced, even eliminated without significantly affecting current combat readiness. The production of military capabilities depends not on capital *investment* in a particular year but on the *stock* of capital in that year. The currently available stock in turn is the result of cumulative effects of capital investment decisions made over several years, even decades in the past. That stock will increase as capital investment is made and will decrease as part of that stock is removed or discarded as it becomes technologically and militarily obsolete. It will thus increase in those years when net capital investment is positive, that is when total or gross investment exceeds the expenditure required to replace that part of the stock which is removed. It will decrease in those years when net investment is negative. Capital investment is therefore a flow having nothing to do with current military capabilities, but it adds to the future stock of capital, which has everything to do with future capabilities. Clearly, then, neglecting capital expenditures, even in a single year, can have implications for reduced military capabilities over a long period of time. It is this flow and stock relationship between capital expenditures and the stock of capital assets which underlies the complex dynamic nature of the defence management challenge.

The fact that the existing stock of capital required many years to accumulate results from both funding constraints and from technical limitations imposed by the long gestation periods associated with acquiring new military assets. Moreover, once in service, these assets, especially expensive weapons systems, are not likely to be replaced very quickly. They will tend to remain in service for very long periods of time. Changing the size or the composition of the capital stock, except in times of national emergency and general mobilization, is therefore always a very long-term proposition. For this reason, defence management, which almost by definition must be concerned with continuous modernization of the capital stock, must adopt a planning horizon of very long-run proportions. In theory at least, this horizon must be sufficiently lengthy to encompass a complete recapitalization of all military assets. Thus, if the average lifespan of military physical assets is, say, 15 years, as is assumed in this paper, then the planning horizon should also be 15 years.

A further complication to the defence management challenge arises out of the complex interdependence among the three categories of budgetary expenditure. The operations and maintenance category turns out to be the key to this complexity. These expenditures, for example, will depend critically on expenditures on personnel. The greater is the size of manpower input, the more will necessarily be spent on operations and maintenance. But within a fixed budget, the more spent on operations and maintenance, the less will be available for both personnel and for capital expenditures. Similarly, operations and maintenance expenditures will depend significantly on the stock of military assets. The greater is the inventory of equipment and physical infrastructure, the more will be spent on operations and maintenance, again reducing the budgetary amounts available for personnel and for capital investment. As a result of this interdependence, decisions with respect to expenditures on one input category will have implications for spending on the others, both currently and in the future.

If operations and maintenance expenditures are the key to the complexity of the budget structuring exercise, they are, as suggested above, also the key to simplifying the analytical problem. Since operations and maintenance expenditures depend on both manpower numbers and on the stock of capital equipment, the defence management problem can really be reduced to a consideration of these two variables. For analytical purposes, it can be reduced to a consideration of the K/L ratio. From this perspective, then, the challenge to defence management is to allocate the defence budget in such a way that the appropriate capital-labour ratio is achieved, bearing in mind that reaching the K can only be obtained through years of appropriate investment expenditures. Obtaining the appropriate K/L ratio then amounts to achieving the maximum defence capability that can be obtained from a given defence budget. More defence capability could only be managed by increasing the defence budget. Generally, though, the appropriate K/L ratio, and hence the distribution of the defence budget, will be independent of the size of the budget.[2]

... and in Practice

Defence budgetary allocations are obviously not made in this way. Nor could they be. First of all, defence does not produce a single homogenous and generalized product called defence capability. It produces many different products with many different production processes. Navies and air forces, for example, have highly capital-intensive production processes. Armies are obviously more labour intensive. Each of these individual services is in turn made up of many subunits each producing its own product and each having its own particular production process. Moreover, some producing units will create more than one defence output. Some outputs, such as joint operations, will require the cooperation of several different producing units.

Despite this complexity, defence budgets have to be allocated. High level decisions, or at least general direction with regard to sharing the budget among personnel, operations and maintenance, and capital expenditures have to be made. In practice, then, two polar approaches to this allocation problem have emerged. These may be tagged respectively as the *arm-the-man* approach and the *man-the-arm* approach. Under the arm-the-man approach, a force size considered to be more or less appropriate to the expected defence budget is decided. What remains after this force is paid and its operating costs looked after is allocated to capital expenditure. The other extreme, the man-the-arm approach, is similar except that the allocation of primary concern becomes capital expenditure while personnel expenditure becomes the residual. With both approaches, in contrast to the rational resource allocation approach discussed above, the distribution of the defence budget will not be independent of the size of the defence budget. With the man-the-arm approach, the allocation will shift in favour of personnel expenditures as the budget grows. With the arm-the-man approach, increased budgets will favour expenditures on capital. Similarly, when defence budgets are not compensated for inflation, the burden of inflation under the arm-the-man approach will be carried by capital expenditures. Under the man-the-arm approach the burden of inflation would fall on manpower expenditures.

There is a natural tendency for both governments and militaries to favour the arm-the-man approach. In the first instance, expenditures for manpower and operations and maintenance provide an immediate return in terms of military capability. The return on capital expenditures will only be felt in the distant future, when it may well be somebody else's responsibility. This bias to heavily discount the future will tend to be particularly strong when there exists a well-established and well-defined threat. Similarly, when budgets are tight or diminishing, it might seem to make sense to favour personnel expenditures and thereby husband manpower resources until such time as looser purse strings might make more room available for capital expenditures. The arm-the-man approach is also favoured, if not mandated by the practice of almost all governments of constraining defence management choices not only by setting the size of the defence budget, but also by establishing manpower levels. A bias in favour of budgetary allocations to manpower may also be found in the persistent tendency to measure military capability and even international stature in terms of the size of armed forces. Finally, since larger forces provide more potential for promotion and for exercising command, senior military managers may be predisposed to favouring personnel expenditures along with operations and maintenance expenditures, again at the expense of capital expenditures.

The man-the-arm approach, as might be expected given the biases in favour of manpower expenditures, is much less usual. It is an approach that puts heavy emphasis on future capabilities. It suggests that military potential is best served by having in place adequate stocks of equipment, including a defence industrial base. Manpower is much less time-dependent than capital and can be acquired relatively quickly should the need arise. But this is likely to be the preferred budgetary approach only under conditions of increasing defence budgets, when adequate resources have been made available to meet both current needs and future needs. To the extent that a nation's defence policy is imbedded in the size and content of its stock of military equipment, it is extremely constrained in its ability to change that policy in the short run. This might also explain the reluctance of government to spend on military capital. Committing to a capital acquisition program is committing to a long-run defence policy. But, in the face of long-run political, economic, and technological uncertainties, governments may well be unwilling to make such commitments.

Conceptually at least, these two alternative approaches to budgetary allocation really represent different approaches to establishing the K/L ratio. Whereas the arm-the-man approach attacks the problem from the denominator, the man-the-arm approach attacks it from the numerator. Nevertheless, these two approaches to defence management have to be recognized as extremes. The actual approach taken in practice will lie somewhere between the two, if for no other reason than that capital-intensive navies and air forces will be less disposed to the arm-the-man approach than will more labour-intensive armies. Therefore, relative political and bureaucratic strengths of the different military services may well affect whether the defence budget distribution is tilted toward manpower or capital expenditures.

THE CANADIAN DEFENCE BUDGET EXPERIENCE

As is evident in Figure 2, a peculiar aspect of Canadian defence spending over the last half-century has been its incredible inertia, in the Newtonian sense of the term. Once started in a particular direction, it continued in that direction until change was unavoidable. Rising rapidly, almost tripling in fact, between 1950 and 1953 to provide for the rearmament needs of the Korean War and NATO obligations in Europe, the defence budget remained approximately at its 1953 level, in nominal

FIGURE 2: Canadian Defence Expenditures 1950-1999

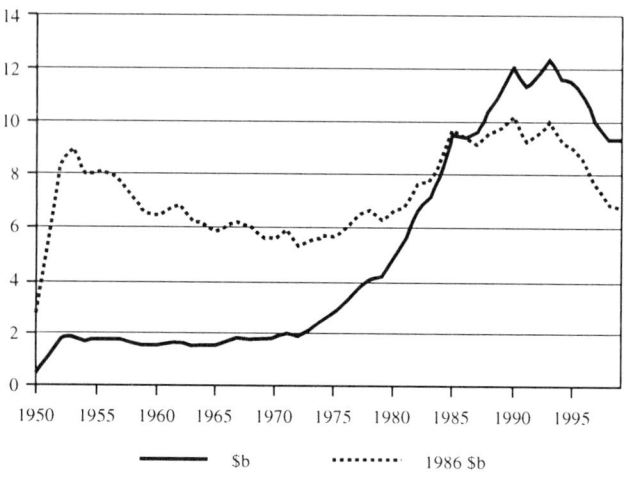

Source: Canada, Department of Finance (various years). Constant dollar expenditures were obtained using the GDP Implicit Price Index (1986 = 100).

terms, for another two decades. It is almost astonishing, in retrospect, to consider that this almost unchanging defence budget withstood the battering of momentous events in the international security environment, in the domestic political environment, in the economy, in military technology, and even in the organization of the Canadian defence establishment. Most significantly, over this period, inflation averaged just under 3 percent per year, which in 20 years reduced real defence expenditure to two-thirds of its 1953 level. As this erosion of defence purchasing power found expression in dramatic changes in the relative balances of manpower and capital available to the military, Canadian defence policy in this period had, in effect, become hostage to the rate of inflation.

By 1973 the inexorable decline in real defence expenditures had reached a crisis stage. Either an already diminished defence establishment would have to be even more drastically reduced, even to the point of irrelevance, or new funding arrangements would have to be made. For a number of reasons, having more to do with political concerns than with military concerns, the latter road was chosen. Thus, from 1973 until 1990 defence expenditures increased at an annual average rate of about 11 percent in nominal terms and about 3.7 percent in real terms. The momentum of these increases through the 1980s was sustained by Canada's adhesion to the NATO undertaking to increase real expenditures by 3 percent per year. Defence expenditures peaked in 1993 at about $12 billion, and remained at approximately that level for another three years. In real terms, however, the defence budget had remained roughly stable at about $10 billion (1986 dollars) from the middle of the 1980s. From this perspective, the 1987 White Paper on defence, with its grandiose expenditure plans, leaves the impression of being a last attempt to continue the moment in defence expenditure increases built up over the past decade. After 1994, however, and another White Paper, defence expenditures began its planned descent toward a level of $9.2 billion by the end of this decade.[3]

The functional distribution of Canadian defence budgets over the past half-century is shown in Figure 3. Clearly evident is the huge buildup in capital expenditures which continued until 1953. After that year, the capital share of the budget declined rapidly, while the shares of operations and maintenance expenditures and personnel expenditures rapidly increased. Equally evident is the crisis period of the early 1970s. By 1973 the proportion of the budget allocated to capital had fallen below 10 percent while personnel expenditures had reached almost two-thirds of the budget. What really made this situation a crisis, however, was that these budgetary reallocations resulted despite the fact that between 1961 and 1973 the size of the armed forces had fallen from a 1961 peak of 126,000 to 82,000 — a decrease of 44,000 or over one-third.

FIGURE 3: Canadian Defence Budget Distributions 1950-1999

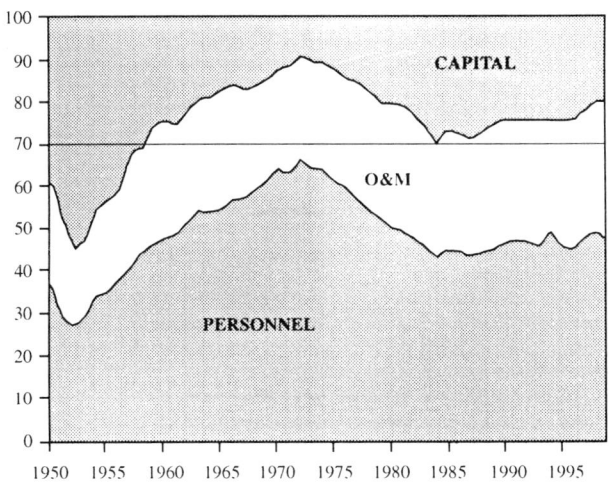

Source: Canada (various years). Transfer payments are excluded.

With the new directions in funding after 1973, it was possible to bring more balance to budgetary allocations. Capital's share rose from the lows of 1973 to almost 30 percent a decade later. In fact, it was in this period that the familiar DND goal of 30 percent emerged, to the best of my knowledge, without any analytical basis. If not analytically derived, however, the idea of 30 percent certainly proved itself as a bureaucratic instrument for improving the capital situation in the department. Indeed, the goal was almost achieved in 1983. (The horizontal line at 70 percent in Figure 3 represents a 30-percent allocation to capital.) In subsequent years, however, this allocation proved unsustainable. As we have seen, in the mid-1980s, though the defence budget was growing at an impressive rate in nominal terms, high rates of inflation rendered it almost stable in real terms. Indeed, after 1983, despite continuing large nominal increases in the defence budget, capital's share of the budget began a slow decline which continues to present day and is forecast to continue until the end of the decade. By contrast, personnel expenditures as a share of the budget have increased modestly while the share going to operations and maintenance has increased somewhat more rapidly. By 1999, the budgetary allocation is predicted to have a distribution ratio of 49-32-19 for personnel, operations and maintenance, and capital respectively.

What clearly emerges from the data on Canadian defence budgets and their distributions is that the resource allocation mechanism within Canadian defence has been based on an arm-the-man approach. Only when defence budgets were rising in real terms, as in the period between 1950 and 1953 and again between 1973 and 1983 did the share of capital increase. Otherwise, and more typically, when defence expenditures were falling, at least in real terms, the share of capital fell. In general then, over the post-World War II period, defence management in Canada has been characterized by attempts to preserve manpower and operations and maintenance expenditures at the expense of capital expenditures. Put differently, the defence management bias has been toward the preservation of forces-in-being at the expense of future or potential forces. As a result, capital expenditures have largely been determined as residual expenditures: what is left over after expenditures on manpower and expenditures on operations and maintenance has been allocated to capital. Equally significantly, capital expenditures have been left to carry the burden of inflation. Understandable as such a bias might be, it suggests that the distribution of Canadian defence budgets depends critically on the size of the budget and not, as economic theory advises it should be, on any desire to achieve appropriate capital-labour ratios. This requires the conclusion that defence budgets have not been optimally distributed, at least in terms of maximizing the defence capability potentially obtainable from the defence budget.

MODELLING FUTURE DEFENCE BUDGETS

The statement that Canadian defence budgets have not been optimally distributed requires a demonstration that there exist alternative and better ways. To attempt this demonstration, we have constructed a simple and rather naive model of defence resource allocation. Unlike the arm-the-man or man-the-arm models of defence resource management, this model takes as its starting point an assumed capital-labour ratio which is desired for some point in the future.[4] A time path for adjusting the current capital-stock ratio to the desired ratio is then defined and the model is solved to describe the time path of personnel expenditures, operations and maintenance expenditures, and capital expenditures. The determining variables for these expenditure categories are the desired capital-labour ratio, the forecast defence budget, and the size of the existing capital stock. It is important to note that, in this model, none of the three expenditure categories is residually determined: rather all three are determined simultaneously.

The capital stock variable is the critical variable in this modelling exercise. Its construction therefore requires some explanation. First, it must be recognized that no measure of the capital stock at the disposal of the Canadian Forces is available. Even if it were, its usefulness in an analysis of this type would be highly suspect, given that market price evaluations of the capital stock, either in terms of historical asset cost or asset replacement cost, would bear little relationship to the current military usefulness of that stock. Therefore we have ventured to look at the capital stock simply as an accumulation over a defined period of past, constant dollar expenditures on capital assets. Thus, our series on capital stock is calculated simply as a moving 15-year total of constant dollar capital expenditures, 15 years being the average life we assumed for military assets. In each year new capital expenditures were added to the previous year's stock while capital expenditures made 16 years ago were deducted from it. If the new capital expenditure exceeded the capital expenditure made 16 years ago, then additions exceed deductions and the capital stock experienced positive growth; if the opposite were true, then deductions exceeded additions and the capital stock declined. There are a number of important theoretical and empirical difficulties with this so-called vintage model of the capital stock. In the first instance, in any given year we are aggregating capital expenditures over many different types of military assets and treating the total expenditure as a homogeneous addition to the capital stock. It implies, for example, that a million dollars spent on a particular type of aircraft and a million dollars spent on, say, trucks represent equivalent additions to the stock of military assets when they may, of course, differ widely in their individual contribution to the production of military capability. There is also a problem with the dating of the acquisition of capital assets. Again, our methodology treats capital assets acquired at different time periods as homogeneous units of capital. Newer equipment, however, even of the same type, will usually embody higher levels of technology than older equipment and logically should not be aggregated into a single measure of capital. Thus, the best that can be said for the measure of capital stock employed in this analysis is that it introduces into the analysis of defence resource allocation problems at least some concern for the effect of past expenditures on durable assets used in the production of defence capability.

In constructing the model, it was necessary, as described previously, to explicitly include a relationship explaining the dependence of operations and maintenance expenditures on both manpower levels and on the level of the capital stock. Our approach to this was to test various regression relationships using operations and maintenance as the dependent variable and manpower and capital stock as the independent variables. In our experiments, the relationship between operations and maintenance expenditures and the level of military manpower was readily evident, significant, and of the appropriate sign. Somewhat surprisingly, however, the effect of the capital stock on operations and maintenance expenditures was manifested not through the size of the capital stock as we had expected, but rather through the average age of the capital stock. Since the age variable was found to have a strongly significant negative coefficient, the implication is that the younger the capital stock, the higher the operations and maintenance expenditures required to support it.

One important omission from this simple model of budgetary allocation is the absence of any treatment of the effects of change in the relative prices of the inputs. In fact, the model implicitly assumes that there will be no changes in the price of military manpower relative to capital over the planning period. As this is not likely to be the case, some discussion of the effects of relative price changes is in order. Economic theory suggests that to maximize the defence capability achieved from a given defence budget, capital, for example, should be substituted for manpower as the price of manpower rises relative to the price of capital. This substitution will lead to a rise in the capital-labour ratio. The amount of change in this ratio will depend upon the technology of producing defence capability.[5] It may be, for example, that the technology of producing defence capability is such that a 10-percent increase in the relative price of manpower requires a 10-percent increase in the capital-labour ratio. In this case, the share of the budget allocated to personnel expenditures would not change since the reduction in manpower acquired would be just offset by the increase in its price. Higher rates of technical substitution in defence would lead to more than proportionate increases in the capital-labour ratio for a given change in relative prices. In these cases the proportion of the budget allocated to personnel expenditures would fall and the proportion allocated to capital would rise. Lower rates of technical substitution would lead to less than proportionate increases in the capital-labour ratio but would require an increase in personnel expenditures at the expense of capital expenditures. To consider one extreme, if the technology of producing defence capability allows no substitution between manpower and capital, that is, the technology of producing defence capability requires that manpower and capital be used in fixed proportions, then there would be no change in the capital-labour ratio as a result of a rise in the relative price of manpower. Maintaining this fixed capital-labour ratio within a fixed defence budget would require, however, an increase in expenditure on manpower and an offsetting reduction in expenditure on capital. In this case, the share of personnel expenditures in the budget would rise at the expense of capital expenditures.

THE STATUS QUO FUTURE

The model described above will generate time-paths for budgetary allocations given a desired capital-labour ratio, a budget level, and the operations and maintenance parameters obtained in the regression analysis. This differs from the arm-the-man model of budgetary allocation characteristic of Canadian defence budgetmaking. In that approach, as described earlier, the planning variable becomes the level of manpower rather than the capital-labour ratio. Capital expenditures are then determined as residual expenditures. The capital-labour ratio, rather than being the major determinant of the budgetary allocations process, emerges as a passive result of that process. To provide a basis for comparison with the results of the rational resource allocation model, we have simulated the time-paths which would result from an arm-the-man budgetary approach for the 15-year planning period beginning in the fiscal year 2000. These simulations represent what we have termed the status quo future. Two versions of this status quo future have been calculated, one that does not include compensation for inflation in the defence budget and one that does.

The broad outline of what defence spending and defence manpower are intended to look like after 1999 are beginning to become clear. Barring a major change in defence policy, it appears that defence expenditures will range between $9 and $10 billion, a level that the current defence minister has suggested is about right for Canada. Manpower levels are already planned to fall to 60,000 by the end of the decade. The critical unknown at this stage is whether, after 1999, defence expenditures will be compensated for inflation. Most defence planning is based on the premise that it will be. But it is instructive to examine the budgetary

FIGURE 4: Status Quo Future Distributions: No Inflation Compensation

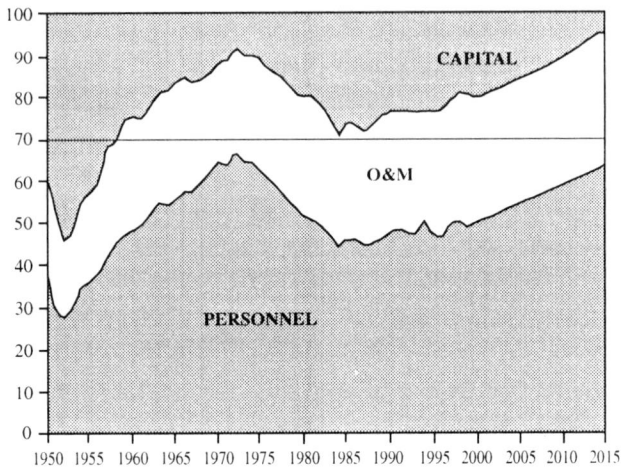

allocation situation should that not be the case. The implications are suggested in Figure 4. Note that what results is a situation not unlike that which occurred in the early 1970s. Toward the end of the planning period, if new funding arrangements are not made, or if manpower is not significantly reduced, capital expenditure would once again be reaching intolerably low levels. By 2015, both the stock of capital and the capital-stock ratio would have fallen to levels typical of the mid-1980s.

Under a budgetary regime that compensates for inflation, the allocation picture, as shown in Figure 5, is considerably improved. On the assumption that the nominal defence budget for the fiscal year 2000-01 will be $10 billion, the distribution of the defence budget would vary little over the planning period. On average, the distribution ratio over the 15-year period would be 49-29-22 for personnel, operations and maintenance, and capital expenditures respectively. Given recent budgetary experience this would not appear to be an unattractive future for defence managers, particularly if it is sustainable. Certainly, it has the appeal of offering considerably more stability and predictability in defence budgeting, and hence in defence planning, than has been the case in the past. The manpower base is preserved at 60,000 and about ten years into the planning period the stock of capital also begins to stabilize. As a result, the capital-labour ratio begins to stabilize at about $0.46 million (1986 dollars) as shown in Figure 6. Interestingly, this

FIGURE 5: Status Quo Future Distributions: Inflation Compensation

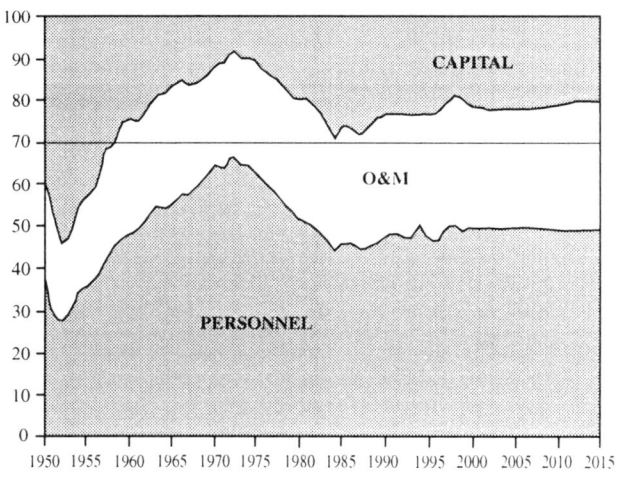

FIGURE 6: Status Quo Future Capital-Labour Ratios

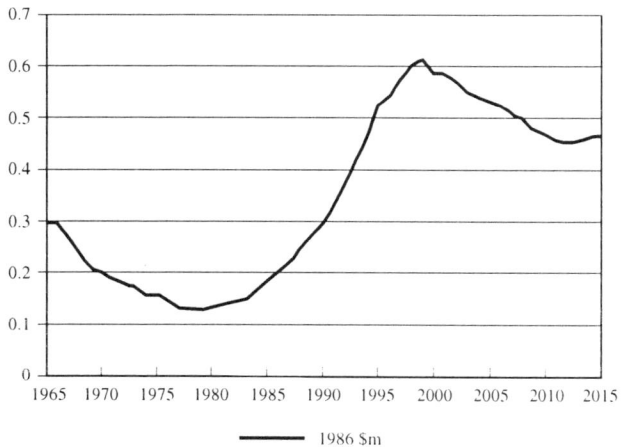

is about the same ratio as that calculated for 1994, the last year before the large reductions in manpower were announced and the year of the last White Paper on defence. The higher capital-labour ratios which existed in the interim may be attributed to an excess of capital stock resulting from investment decisions taken in the 1980s and reflecting the manpower planning levels of that period.

Stability and predictability in funding are certainly desirable attributes in any defence management environment. However, the question must still be asked whether this is the best way to spend $10 billion for Canadian defence. In particular one has to question whether the mix of manpower and capital which emerges in this status quo future is the appropriate mix for war fighting in the early decades of the next century. There are reasons to suspect that it does not. Since this future results in a declining and then stabilizing capital stock in combination with a stable manpower level, the focus of defence planning over this period will necessarily be on capital replacement and not on capital deepening. The capital replacement mentality, represented by the emerging stable capital-labour ratios, would permit only marginal improvements in the technological capability of the forces. Increased technological capability requires capital deepening, such that military personnel are on average increasingly well-equipped, and would require increasing capital-labour ratios. The capital-labour ratio which emerges in the latter years of the planning period for the status quo future is about 50 percent higher than that which existed in 1965, a half-century earlier. But in that interim the technology of war fighting has undergone a number of revolutions, each one leading to a more capital-intensive technology. We have seen this in recent years in the appearance of precision-guided weapons, stealth technology, and highly sophisticated command, control and communications systems, including the intensifying use of information technology. Such trends are very likely going to continue and to accelerate in the decades ahead. Indeed, reference is now made not so much to trends in military technology but rather to a revolution in military affairs (*The Economist*, pp. 21-23; and Bodnar 1993). It is predictable, therefore, that the capital-labour ratios that emerge in the status quo future, stable though they may be, are going to prove inadequate for the defence realities of the next century.

Apart from technological developments, there is a strategic reason to expect that more capital deepening will be required. With the end of the Cold War and the loss of definition of the threat, defence planning must now come to grips with high degrees of uncertainty about where, when, with whom, against whom, and how military operations will have to take place in the future. Under these circumstances, and also because greater uncertainty must now be met by smaller forces, defence planning must emphasize flexibility, adaptiveness, and mobility. Reshaping military forces to become more flexible, more adaptive, and more mobile would seem to require investments in equipment that go beyond the mere replacement of existing equipment.

ALTERNATIVE FUTURES

Without complete knowledge of the technology of defence and complete knowledge about the relative costs of the defence inputs, it is impossible to say just what the appropriate capital-labour ratio should be. However, assuming that it should be increased to some level, as argued above, then it is meaningful to ask how the defence budget should be allocated among personnel expenditures, operations and maintenance expenditures, and capital expenditures to achieve that ratio over a given period of time? To explore this question we use our model to examine two alternative futures. The first, which we term the high recapitalization future, assumes that the capital-labour ratio will rise from the expected 1999-2000 level of $0.6 million constant 1986 dollars to a value of $1 million constant 1986 dollars by the year 2015 as shown in Figure 7. This very high level of the capital-labour ratio may be taken as being suggestive of Canada's fully buying into the revolution in military affairs. As in the simulation of the status quo future, the year 2000 is taken as the start point since the budgetary plan is already fairly well known up to that year. Again, since a complete recapitalization could reasonably

FIGURE 7: High Recapitalization Future Capital and Manpower Levels

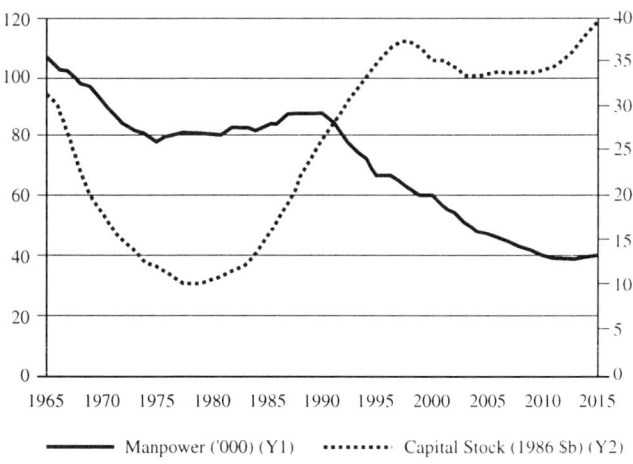

be expected to take about 15 years, the year 2015 is taken as the end point. Together these assumptions imply that the capital-labour ratio grows at an annual rate of 3.5 percent. The defence budget for 2000-01 is assumed, as previously, to be $10 billion and is to be fully compensated for inflation over the planning period.

The results of this experiment are shown in Figures 7 and 8. Achieving a capital-labour ratio of $1 million (constant 1986 dollars) in 2015 requires that the capital stock grows to about $40 billion (1986 dollars) in that year. To provide the room for the capital expenditures required to grow the capital stock to this level, manpower would have to continue to fall below 60,000 until it reached an equilibrium level of about 40,000 in the year 2015. To achieve this trade-off between manpower and capital, a reallocation of the defence budget would be required as shown in Figure 8. After the year 2000, there would be a continuing increase in the budget share going to capital as well as in the share going to operations and maintenance. These increases would be compensated by a decreasing share for personnel. By 2015 the distribution of the defence budget would be in the proportions 33-32-35 for personnel, operations and maintenance, and capital respectively.

This high capitalization future may be too rich and too revolutionary. Certainly there would be widespread opposition to the idea of reducing the manpower level to 40,000 particularly when the status quo future seems to provide a budgetary allocation profile that differs little from those of countries of similar situation. It is useful, therefore, to consider the budgetary implications of an intermediate

FIGURE 8: High Recapitalization Future Budget Distributions

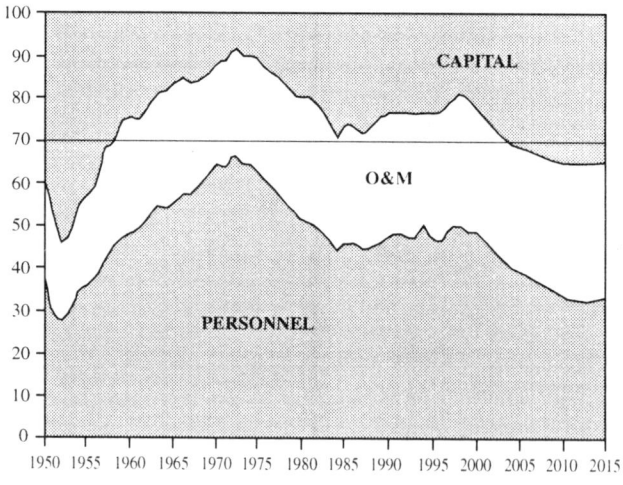

future, one that involves a somewhat more moderate recapitalization of the Canadian Forces. An appropriate level might be $0.6 million (1986 dollars). This represents a capital-labour ratio which is 50 percent greater than that obtained in 1993 and twice the ratio obtained in 1965. Moreover, it is approximately the level to be reached in 1999-2000 under current funding and manpower plans. Achieving that level would therefore require no growth in the capital-labour ratio after that year. Importantly, too, it would permit no decline after that year. The capital-labour ratio would therefore remain fixed at $0.6 million (1986 dollars) throughout the planning period.

The results of this moderate capitalization experiment are shown in Figures 9 and 10. As in the high recapitalization future, maintaining a capital-labour ratio of 0.6 would also require a drop in manpower levels. In this intermediate case, manpower levels would drop to a low of about 50,500 in 2011 but would rise again to about 55,000 in 2015. Personnel expenditures would change accordingly, as indicated in Figure 10, and these would be offset by changes in expenditures for capital. Capital expenditures would rise to a maximum of 28 percent of the budget in 2010 before falling again to 24 percent in 2015. In the final year of the planning period the distribution of the defence budget would be in the ratio 45-31-24 for personnel expenditures, operations and maintenance expenditures, and capital expenditures respectively. This compares with the 49:32:19 ratio obtained under the status quo future.

FIGURE 9: Moderate Recapitalization Future Capital and Manpower Levels

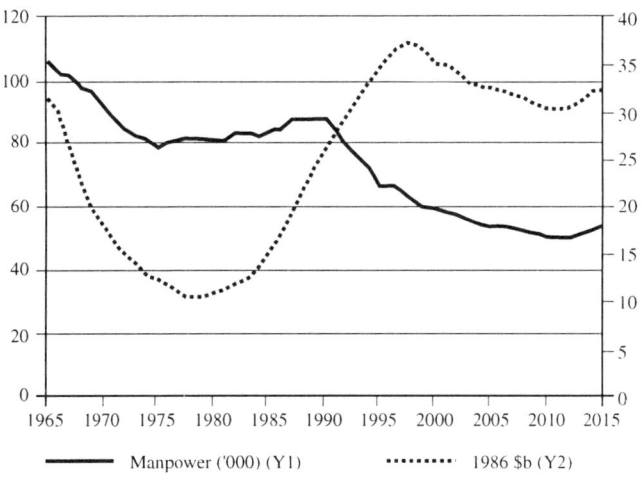

FIGURE 10: Moderate Recapitalization Future Budget Distribution

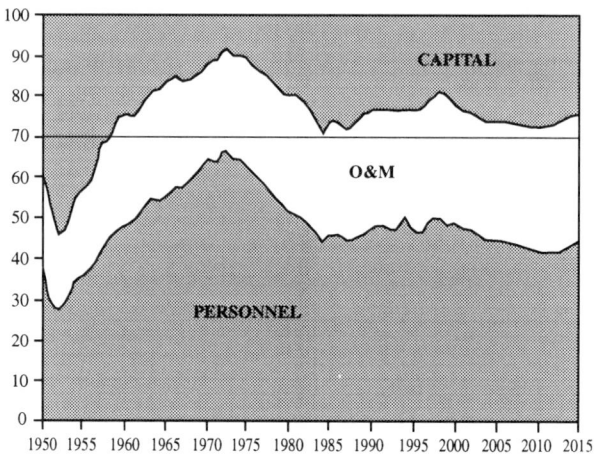

Comparing the status quo future with the two alternative futures identifies the sorts of trade-offs that defence management must deal with. In 2015 the status quo future preserves the 60,000 manpower level. The high capitalization future requires a reduction to about 40,000. In return for this one-third reduction in manpower, the capital-labour ration increases from 0.45 to one million 1986 dollars, or roughly double. The appropriate question to be addressed by defence management is the following: Is a one-third reduction in manpower worth a 100 percent increase in how well equipped this smaller force would be? Similarly, comparing the status quo future with the moderate recapitalization future suggests that a reduction to a manpower level in 2015 would permit a 50-percent increase in the capital-labour ratio. Is a 10-percent reduction in manpower worth a 50-percent increase in how well equipped the smaller force would be?

It is perhaps of some interest, and certainly useful in driving home the nature of the trade-off issues involved in defence resource allocation problems, to apply the model to a slightly different issue. Assuming an average annual rate of inflation of 2 percent, the $10 billion constant-dollar budget assumed for the period after 1999 would represent a nominal dollar expenditure of close to $13 billion in 2015. What inflation-compensated budget would be required in 2015 to provide both the capital-labour ratios assumed under these two alternative futures and a manpower level of 60,000? For the moderate recapitalization future, the model suggests that the required defence budget would be $21.3 billion, or about 50 percent higher than the expected 2015 budget. For the high recapitalization future, the required budget in 2015 would be about $56 billion, or over four times the expected budget.

CONCLUSIONS

The primary purpose of the paper was to explore the basic logic of making defence budgetary choices. The approach was to contrast practical defence budgetmaking with budgetmaking based on some basic economic ideas of rationality in production. Under the latter approach, choices about inputs into the defence production process are made under a fixed budget such that personnel expenditures and capital investment expenditures are chosen so as to achieve a desired capital-labour ratio at some particular point in time. In this approach, the capital-labour ratio, which simply represents how well on average the military forces are equipped, becomes the critical design variable in defence budgetmaking. Just which capital-labour ratio would lead to maximizing the defence capability obtained out of a given defence budget depends both on the technology of making defence capabilities and on the relative costs of defence inputs. Adjusting the desired capital-labour ratio over time will require a reallocation of defence expenditures between capital and manpower and hence a changing budgetary distribution between personnel expenditures, operations and maintenance expenditures, and capital expenditures. As illustrated in the two alternative futures discussed in the paper, the time-path of these allocations will depend upon the expected defence budget, the initial manpower level and the inherited stock of military assets. Accordingly, the appropriate budgetary allocation to capital expenditures can only be determined once these conditions are specified. These experiments also suggest that it is inappropriate to speak in terms of a particular target percentage for capital expenditures, or for any other defence input expenditure, since a steady state of stable budgetary allocations is achievable only in the long run. The important thing would seem to be to attempt to structure defence budgets in terms of time paths of distributions defined to achieve an appropriate ratio of capital assets to manpower.

By contrast, practical approaches to defence budgeting are usually based on selecting a given level of one of the inputs, usually manpower, as the point of departure in making budgetary allocations. Given a fixed defence budget, other budgetary categories are then determined residually. Under this approach, the capital-labour ratio emerges as the result of budgetary allocations rather than being the primary determinant of those allocations. This has obvious implications for the misallocation of defence resources between current operations and future capabilities, especially as these misallocations are manifested in more, but inadequately equipped troops. If Canadian experience is any guide, this approach also has the potential to create budgetary crises. In emphasizing stability in the structure of defence budgets, it engenders, as argued in the paper, rigidities in dealing with the trade-off between forces-in-being and future forces. These rigidities in turn can lead to short-run considerations of funding current operations coming to dominate long-run consideration of providing for future forces. This can occur, and has occurred to such a degree that changing relative costs and inflation can slowly but inevitably erode the stock of military assets to such a point where the continuing operational capability of the military forces is called into question. The distortions caused by crises of this sort can leave an enduring impact on defence capabilities. It can lead, for example, to a defence management environment where the principal concern is for the preservation of a minimum stock of capital and not with the growth of this stock. This can lead to a defence management perennially locked into a capital replacement psychology, with at best only marginal improvements being made to capabilities. It is to become locked into a budgetary structure that resists change and becomes increasingly out of phase with the requirements of modern war fighting. It is to foster mediocrity with a continuing search for a non-existent stability and predictability in defence budgets.

The model used to arrive at these conclusions crudely oversimplifies the very complex reality of defence decisionmaking. For one thing, it is much too aggregative. Making defence cannot be described in terms of a single technology; rather there are many different defence outputs contributing to overall defence capability and each one of these will have its own technology. Therefore, were the data available, it would be much more interesting to build up a budgetary allocation model based on the different production realities of the three services, or even of individual defence activities. Another major difficulty with the model lies in the definition and measurement of the capital stock variable. Everything else in the model depends upon this variable, but in its construction a number of important theoretical and empirical difficulties have been quite cavalierly passed over. But perhaps the major difficulty with the model is to be found in the treatment of the manpower variable. Manpower in our model is treated simply as a flow variable. In reality, however, the military invests huge sums every year in the education and training of military personnel. In doing so they acquire a stock of human capital, and there can be little doubt that in the future, at least, if the technology of producing military capability in any way reflects the technology of production in general, this stock of human capital will become the most important defence input. Properly, then, a model of defence budgetary allocation should include manpower not only as a flow variable but also as a stock of human capital. Explicit consideration would then have to be given to budgetary trade-offs between investment in physical capital and investment in human capital, the latter in the form of resources allocated to education and training.

Despite these inadequacies, dealing with questions of defence budgeting in terms of simple economic models forces us to come to grips with concepts of defence output and defence inputs. It also forces us to conceptualize about the relationships between inputs and outputs and to attempt to think about these relationships in a time-dependent way such that we might make a little more sense out of the real world of managing defence budgets.

NOTES

1. The defence management problem could also be described as selecting that combination of inputs which minimizes the budget required to produce a given level of military capability. The American approach to the determination of defence budgets appears to come close to this model. Defence capability is defined in terms of winning two major regional conflicts at approximately the same time. The level of the defence budget and its structure are then determined and structured, at least in theory, to achieve this capability at minimum cost.
2. Technically, independence between the size of the budget and the optimal K/L ratio requires that the defence production function be homothetic.
3. The 1997-98 Estimates for National Defence indicate planned total appropriated expenditures of $9.4 billion for the fiscal year 1998-99 and $9.7 billion for fiscal year 1999-2000. Because we are primarily interested in defence as a production activity, we define total defence spending as the sum of expenditures for personnel, operations and maintenance, and capital. Thus we ignore transfer payments made out of the defence budget as well as revenues credited to the defence votes. As a result, our totals for 1998-99 and 1999-2000 are $9.5 billion and $9.8 billion respectively.
4. The optimum capital-labour ratio is theoretically determined by the relative marginal productivities of manpower and capital and by their relative prices. In this exercise we assume no change in relative prices of the inputs and simply postulate that there exists a desired capital-labour ratio.
5. Technically, substitution response to changes in relative price changes are described by the elasticity of technical substitution. When this value is equal to one, changes in relative prices will leave expenditure on each input unchanged as a given percentage change in price is just offset by an equal and opposite percentage change in the quantity purchased. Higher elasticities will lead to reductions in expenditure on the relatively more expensive input and increased expenditures on the relatively less expensive input. For elasticities less than one, that is where there is less opportunity of substitution between the inputs, the quantity of the relatively more expensive input will decrease but not sufficiently to offset the percentage increase in price and thus expenditure on that input will increase. All of these cases would require some change in the capital-labour ratio to maximize defence output of a fixed budget. However, for an elasticity equal to zero, the inputs are perfect compliments and must be used in fixed proportions. There are therefore no substitution possibilities. An increase in the price of one input relative to the other will cause expenditure on that input to increase, but there will no change in the capital-labour ratio.

REFERENCES

Bodnar, J.W. (1993), "The Military Technical Revolution: From Hardware to Information," *Naval War College Review*, 46 (3):343.

Canada (1995), *1995-96 Estimates, National Defence Part III, Expenditure Plan*, Ottawa: Supply and Services Canada.

_____ (1996), *1996-97 Estimates, National Defence Part III, Expenditure Plan*, Ottawa: Supply and Services Canada.

_____ (1997), *1997-98 Estimates, National Defence Part III, Expenditure Plan*, Ottawa: Supply and Services Canada.

_____ (various years), *Estimates of the Government of Canada*, Ottawa: Supply and Services Canada.

Canada, Department of Finance (various years), *Economic Reference Tables*, Ottawa: Supply and Services Canada.

Canada, Department of National Defence (1964), *White Paper on Defence*, Ottawa: Queen's Printer.

_____ (1992), *Statement on Canadian Defence Policy by the Honourable Marcel Masse*, Ottawa: Supply and Services Canada.

The Economist (1997), "The Future of Warfare," 8 March, pp. 21-23.

CHAPTER FIVE

Education in Defence Resources Management: The Next Decade

John E. Dawson
Charles J. LaCivita

INTRODUCTION

Consider the following reports:

1. *The Naval Postgraduate School (NPS) Fire Department*: During a lecture to the Senior International Defense Management Class at the Defense Resources Management Institute in July 1996, Rear Admiral Marsha Evans, superintendent of NPS and director of the Institute, mentioned that she had caused "quite a flap" by proposing to reduce the number of firemen per truck at the NPS fire department from four to three. She pointed out that NPS is a reinvention laboratory, and this was only one of her proposals. Some consideration had been given to outsourcing the Fire Department. However, it was noted that all the surrounding community fire departments had three firemen per truck, while the NPS, following navy regulations has four. She proposes following local community standards (methods and training) as a way to save resources.

2. *Empty Buildings at Norfolk Naval Base*: A private company, in Norfolk, VA, wanted to rent one of the Navy's sagging, "temporary" buildings here. It offered $400,000 a year for a Cold War relic that was sitting empty.
"We can't do that! Tear it down," ordered Admiral William J. "Bud" Flanagan Jr., commander of the Atlantic Fleet and the short, stocky czar of the sprawling Norfolk Naval Base.
The admiral, who oversees an $11 billion budget but spent many of his 29 years in the Navy hunting for Soviet submarines, had reason to torpedo the deal. He had hired an outside research firm to analyze the base's $100 million energy

bill — a first — and found that heating and cooling the 70,000 square-foot, uninsulated structure would cost nearly $1 million a year. So the rental would lose money. Now, the building is the 84th that the admiral has ordered destroyed, and he has targeted 80 more (*Wall Street Journal*, 19 August 1996, p. 1).

3. *The Massachusetts Department of Motor Vehicles*: If you are clocked doing 85 mph on the Mass. Pike, now you can pay for it while doing 28,800 bps on the Internet. Massachusetts has become the first state to allow motorists to pay speeding fines and other non-criminal violations via the WorldWideWeb.

With the ticket number and a credit card at hand, violators "surf" to the Massachusetts Registry of Motor Vehicles at http://www.state.ma.us/rmy and pay for their sins. The Web site, which was developed for $50,000, also allows motorists to conduct common transactions such as renewing car registrations. More services will become Web-friendly, including ordering vanity plates.

It is all part of the bay state's continuing drive to eliminate the endless lines that snarled its offices a few years back — a cause several other states have adopted, although not yet by allowing transactions via the Web. "This will help us meet our goal, which is never to see another customer again," says a spokesman, half-jokingly. Through the Internet service, the state hopes eventually to cut back on some of its $46 million annual DMV budget (*Business Week*, 19 August 1996, p. 6).

4. *The Internal Revenue Service*: CYBERFLOP? An IRS attempt to expand electronic filing draws more criticism. The General Accounting Office (GAO), a congressional-watchdog agency, has found big problems with "Cyberfile," a proposed system to let taxpayers prepare and send their returns electronically using personal computers without having to pay a transmission fee. A GAO report to a congressional committee calls the Cyberfile project "poorly planned and managed." One GAO official calls the report "very hard-hitting."

Early in 1997, the GAO disclosed that the Internal Revenue Service (IRS) had delayed the start of its pilot program, and went on to say that a review of the new system found "many of the management and technical weaknesses" that even senior Treasury officials acknowledge have bedevilled IRS efforts to modernize (*The Wall Street Journal*, 4 September 1966, p. 1).

Are these simply isolated events or are they indicative of a major shift in attention by executives in the public sector — federal, state, and local — including the Department of Defense? We argue that it is the latter. A quick way of characterizing this change is that the strategic process is becoming more *periodic*, while the operating process is becoming more *immediate*. In many ways, it is reminiscent of the 1950s when technical efficiency in the performance of public services was the dominant focus in public sector resources management. By contrast, the 1960s opened an era of almost hectic attention to policy and the development of new approaches and systems — in domestic programs as well as defence. The 1970s and 1980s were more of a mix of some policy initiatives, some attempts to improve existing programs, and mainly considerable disappointment on both dimensions. Meanwhile, beginning in the 1980s, US business got very serious about performance through downsizing and restructuring. What business has been doing the last decade and a half is beginning to be "where the action is" in government. This, we argue, calls for a change in emphasis in education in resources management.

DEFENCE RESOURCES MANAGEMENT FROM THE END OF WWII TO THE FALL OF THE BERLIN WALL

World War II was followed by two major developments in US national security. One was the movement to unify the military services into one defence establishment; the second was the retention of large standing forces during peacetime.

The Unification of the US Military Departments

The evolution of strategy during WWII called for the services to fight jointly. This led to the movement to unify the services, a development that they, particularly the Navy, resisted. Nevertheless, the *National Security Act* of 1947 separated the air forces from the Army and combined all of the services into the National Military Establishment, the precursor of the US Department of Defense. In addition, in the Key West Agreement of 1948, the services divvied up the roles and missions the military departments were to perform.

Large Standing Forces in Peacetime

The onset of the Cold War led the US, for the first time in its history, to retain large standing forces in "peacetime," including forces predeployed in both Europe and Asia. In addition, it launched an era of military technological and intelligence competition with the USSR which, with the new threat of nuclear war, added a sense of frenetic urgency to the formulation of defence strategy and the development of the forces to implement it. This environment highlighted two deficiencies in the defence planning process: the mismatch between plans and budgets and the lack of coordination among the military departments in designing an overall strategy. This environment gave birth to a major innovation in public resources management — the *Planning, Programming, and Budgeting System* (PPBS) introduced in 1961.

The Development of the PPBS

The essentials of the resource allocation problem can be expressed as follows:

$$\text{Inputs} \rightarrow \text{Outputs} \rightarrow \text{Outcomes}$$

Inputs (resources) are converted into outputs that act on the external environment to produce outcomes, that is, desired results. Many difficult decisions must be made to accomplish this seemingly simple task. A country must decide how much of its resources (inputs) to allocate for defence. It must also decide how the resources will be allocated within defence: Which outputs will be produced, and how will they be produced?

Prior to PPBS, military planners and budgeteers approached this process from different perspectives. The planners were most concerned with the threat and focused on the outcomes to be achieved with little regard for the budget. They began with an assessment of the threat, devised a policy and strategy to meet that threat, determined the force structure necessary to carry out the strategy, and totalled the cost of those forces to arrive at a budget, which they hoped the country would finance. That is,

$$\text{Threat} \rightarrow \text{Policy/Strategy} \rightarrow \text{Forces} \rightarrow \text{Budget}$$

Budgeteers, on the other hand, focused primarily on the budget, that is, the cost of the inputs. They started with the overall budget, determined how many forces could be bought, modified the strategy as necessary and hoped that would meet the threat. That is,

$$\text{Threat} \leftarrow \text{Policy/Strategy} \leftarrow \text{Forces} \leftarrow \text{Budget}$$

Rarely did these two approaches yield the same result.

Another problem was that each military service planned as though it were solely responsible for the country's defence. In the 1950s, this meant that each service gave highest priority to the development of nuclear weapons. The second priority was for the main offensive systems each service used in conventional warfare. This led to the priorities presented by Table 1 for each service.

The PPBS provided a means for linking plans and budgets from a Department of Defense (DoD) perspective by advocating programming as the bridge between plans and budgets and the use of analytical techniques as an essential part of the process. In order to decide which programs should be funded, PPBS imposed a DoD perspective rather than a military-service perspective by categorizing forces in a way that linked programs and missions to desired outcomes. This is shown in Table 2.

TABLE 1: Warfare Systems

Army	Navy	Air Force
Ballistic missiles	Ballistic missiles	Ballistic missiles, bombers
Helicopters	Carrier groups	Fighters
Predeployed forces	Cargo ships	Cargo aircraft
R&D	R&D	R&D
Reserves	Reserves	Reserves

TABLE 2: Relationship of DoD and Service Programs

DoD	Army	Navy	Air Force
Strategic forces	Ballistic missiles	Ballistic missiles	Ballistic missiles, bombers
Conventional Forces	Helicopters	Carrier groups	Fighters
Airlift/Sealift	Predeployed forces	Cargo ships	Cargo aircraft
R&D	R&D	R&D	R&D
Reserves	Reserves	Reserves	Reserves

The program structure encouraged both inter- and intra-program trade-offs and connected plans and budgets:

$$\text{Threat} \leftrightarrow \text{Policy/Strategy} \leftrightarrow \text{Forces} \leftrightarrow \text{Budget}$$
$$\searrow \text{Analysis, Risk Assessment} \nearrow$$

Analytical methods were used to reconcile the threat, forces, and the budget. Thus, analysis became crucial to the operation of the system, and PPBS encouraged the use of analysis at each step of the process: planning, implementation, and operating.

The groundwork for this system and for the use of analysis in allocating defence resources was laid in the 1950s and culminated with the publication of Hitch and McKean's *The Economics of Defense in the Nuclear Age* (1960). Addressing the basic problem illustrated above, they showed how analytical methods can aid in deciding which outputs to produce and how to combine inputs to produce outputs.

One of the major problems in deciding which outputs to produce is that the effectiveness of a system is never really known until it is used. Yet, if deterrence is adequate, the system will never be used. This was particularly true of nuclear systems during the Cold War. It is not practical to have a practice nuclear war! Hitch and McKean advocated the use of cost-effectiveness analysis to choose among rival systems. They also addressed the problem of how to combine inputs to produce outputs by adapting the microeconomic production model to defence.

Knowledge Required

This approach to allocating defence resources requires familiarity with material drawn from economics, decision science, and management systems. From economics, the ideas of economy and efficiency, marginal reasoning, and opportunity costs are developed. From decision sciences comes model building and probability and statistics. From management systems comes organizational design and behaviour and management information systems. These ideas are blended into a way of thinking that emphasizes the use of *systems analysis* to help develop strategies and objectives, *program analysis* centred on the use of cost-effectiveness techniques to choose among alternatives and *operational analysis* centred on the microeconomic production function to obtain economy and efficiency in operations.

Cost-effectiveness analysis requires knowledge of how to measure effectiveness and cost. Measuring effectiveness in the absence of war requires the development of criteria based on perceived situations (scenarios) and the outcomes that the system is designed to achieve. Measuring cost means using cost-estimating techniques to estimate the total life-cycle cost of each alternative. This requires knowledge of different types of cost and of the statistical techniques needed to estimate them. Operational analysis requires knowledge of production economics. One must be able to identify and measure outputs and assign costs to those outputs.

From its inception in the 1960s until the end of the Cold War, the main focus of resource allocation was on strategic and programmatic issues. Operational issues were mostly an afterthought and received much less attention. For example, in the 1960s, defence faced an immense challenge to develop strategies and forces to deter nuclear war and conventional war (or at least delay its escalation to nuclear war) on a global basis. Consequently, they focused their attention on the major decisions leading to the acquisition of new systems. Reducing the operating costs of defence was a by-product — as more effective new systems were procured to replace inferior existing systems. That is, cost-effectiveness analysis was much more important than operational analysis.

The Airlift-Sealift program provides an excellent example of the decision environment of the early 1960s. The major airlift program underway was the procurement of the C-141. Upon analysis, it was found that this essentially civilian cargo aircraft was poorly designed for military use. The solution was to insert a "plug" into the fuselage that would lengthen the plane by several feet. When it was determined that this change would delay the plane by a year, the decision was made to go ahead without fixing the design because of the perceived urgency to have greater capability for mobility as soon as possible. Beyond this initial decision, the analysis started with the fundamental question: "Do early and heavy deployments lead to shorter, less costly wars?" After the joint chiefs of staff quantified its positive response to that strategic question, existing systems of mobility were examined and compared with entirely innovative alternatives (C-5 aircraft and roll on-roll off ships). The operating costs most sharply addressed were those of future wars; however, the "spillover" cost advantages of peacetime use also were calculated. Minor tinkering with the present peacetime operating costs of present systems received scant attention. Scarce analytic time was devoted to the replacement of existing systems — not to the fine-tuning of their current costs. It made sense to tolerate current costs of obsolete systems enroute to their replacement.

THE CURRENT ENVIRONMENT

The Rising Importance of Operations

Today, the decision environment is dramatically different. While it remains a dangerous world with sufficient complexity and uncertainty to merit superb analysis in the formulation of strategy and selection of forces, US existing capability is awesome relative to near-term potential demands. There is not the urgency of a bipolar military competition that rationalized buying an inferior C-141. The first major overall assessment of the force structure initiated in the post-Cold War environment was made in 1990 by the Senate Armed Services Committee. Senator Nunn requested information regarding alternative reductions of 15 percent, 25 percent, and 35 percent over the next several years. After examination, the committee chose the 25 percent alternative; it became embodied in the congressional budgeting proposals and accepted by the president several months later. The next major assessment was the bottom-up review conducted in 1993-94 that has framed the defence budget during the following years. The most current assessment scheduled, the quadrennial strategic review, has just been completed. This more *periodic* approach to the big issues offers one of the long-sought goals of most of the players — greater stability to the defence program. And, it offers the potential of some reduction in the workload associated with past defence decision processes (with possible modifications to PPBS procedures). Momentarily at least, the United States does not have a global competitor with the capability to force a technological and structural "race" that would justify the constant and at times frantic pressure identified with the hundreds of program change proposals (PCPs) that symbolized the PPBS process in the early 1960s. A "rolling" Future Years' Defence Program (FYDP) with updates several times within a fiscal year implies a pace of decisionmaking more vigorous than the present *strategic* decision environment requires.

Similarly, the pace of new acquisitions is slowing as the lessened threat environment weakens their rationale and the federal budgetary situation weakens their support. The defence buildup in the 1980s may be sunk costs, but the huge budget deficits, generated by "borrowing" the defence buildup rather than paying for it, remain a very unsunk obstacle to resources available for defence. The 1960s' approach to lowering operating costs (by replacing the old with the new) can be expected to accomplish much less in the future simply because the pace of replacement has lessened. Hence, *micro efforts to improve current operating costs* of existing forces, and most especially of the support systems of existing forces, become very advantageous. Yes, three firemen on a truck rather than four matters! Suddenly, small changes to enhance performance and/or reduce costs become significant when existing force and support systems may have longer lives, implying greater opportunities for repetitive savings to accumulate. And, it may be the major available way to generate funds for new systems when overall defence expenditures are severely constrained.

Evidence of this new environment is showcased in the secretary of defence's annual report to Congress, March 1996:

- In strategic forces, funding in then-year dollars is down from $18 billion in 1990 to $8 billion in 1995, while Operations is up from 38% to 66% of the reduced total (pp. 216-17).

- In aviation forces, both Navy/Marine Corps and Air Force fighter/attack aircraft were at current inventory requirements in 1995, and there is no severe shortfall until after 2010 (pp. 182-83). However, average age in both forces is shown as rising in the near future (p. 179) and new aircraft are required in a next cycle of tactical aircraft procurement (p. 180).

- In mobility forces, strategic airlift capacity is shown in steady state as the C-17 replaces the C-141 (p. 193); strategic sealift is shown reaching required capacity in the year 2000 (p. 195). (Perry 1996.)

Perhaps the most revealing figure shows the Defence Manpower Trend (Figure 1). Active duty military (end strength), primarily assigned to the combatant force programs, had roughly completed its drawdown by FY1995; by contrast, the drawdown in defence civilians (workyears), primarily assigned to the support and administrative programs, remained very much a task yet to be completed. While the civilian reduction from 1989 through 1995 is approximately 24 percent, there is still another 11 percent of the 1989 total yet to be accomplished through FY 2001.

FIGURE 1: Defence Manpower Trend

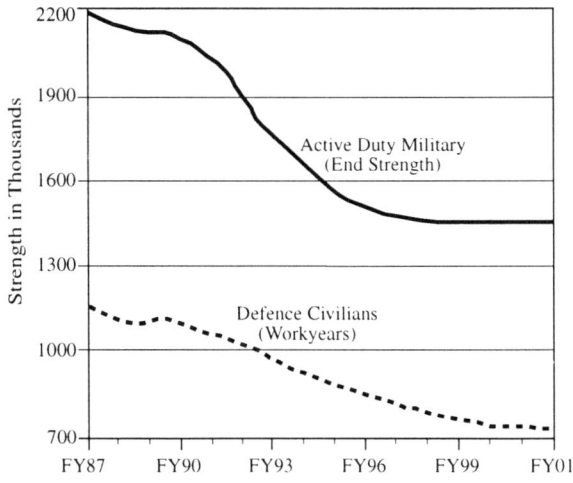

Source: Perry (1996).

The implications for *defence resources management* are illustrated throughout the chapter on Financial Management (Perry 1996, pp. 103-09) and the task is neatly summarized in the conclusion to that chapter:

> Financial management in the Department of Defense is a work in progress. There have been notable successes, but progress is slow in some areas. It is impossible to reverse decades-old problems overnight, and some reforms will require several years of transition, experimentation, re-engineering, and modernization.... In moving ahead, DOD financial management reform must accommodate two unavoidable constraints.

First, the Department cannot stop its financial operations while it fixes outdated business practices and flawed systems. Every day, the Department must manage payrolls, process payments, and produce financial reports. These daily operating requirements impose a strong practical test on all plans for changing systems and business practices. A second constraint is that lasting reform demands consensus and collaboration. Few solutions rest exclusively within the jurisdiction of the financial management community. Reform of DOD financial management invariably entails changes in the business practices of other defense organizations and functional groups — like the acquisition or logistics communities. This demands an unusual degree of consensus building and collaboration, which slows the pace of change. But there is no viable shortcut. Pressing ahead without consensus and collaboration will not produce lasting reform.

DOD's current leadership is committed to making financial management reform a hallmark of its stewardship. Progress to date has been substantial, and the Department is determined to complete this historically significant challenge.

The Message. Defence management has to continue to operate the "going store" while changing how the store operates. Improvements in one area impinge on, and depend on, changes in other areas. It is not a process of simply ordering that it be done. It takes consensus and collaboration to bring authentic reforms.

The new emphasis on operations is borne out by looking at the major innovations in defence resources management since 1989. All have focused on operational issues, especially on the support establishment. In the DoD, we have had initiatives to close bases, implement unit-cost budgeting and revolving funds for spare parts and industrial-type activities, and consolidation of many support systems such as finance and accounting, etc. Moreover, the *Government Performance Results Act* has mandated a government-wide effort to reduce the cost of providing government services. As in defence, the Act focuses on how the government operates, not on what it does. Now, all the departments of the executive, including defence, are "re-engineering," learning business process improvement, developing performance measures, trying to figure out how to do activity-based costing, and wrestling with the out-sourcing of support activities to the private sector. These initiatives are not limited to the US. Similar measures have been undertaken by countries around the world. For example, the UK has already privatized its military housing. This emphasis on operations clearly calls for a different focus and the use of different analytical tools.

Knowledge Required

The current environment requires resource managers to be much more acquainted with business-like practices. An understanding of production economics is needed to understand how costs behave when changes in inputs and input levels are made. Consideration of depreciation and overhead, basically ignored in the past, are important when trying to determine the cost of an output and whether the provision of that output should be out-sourced. This makes a familiarity with cost accounting concepts important. Operations analysis is important when applying restructuring and re-engineering to operations.

Another area that has increased in relative importance is human behaviour and its influence on organizational change. In the past, the emphasis on strategy and new systems meant that the majority of analysis and decisionmaking was conducted by relatively few people at the highest levels of the defence organization. The current emphasis on operations, in contrast, requires participation by all levels of the organization. Hence, designing the behavioural implementation of new procedures and processes as well as the reform of current processes is much more important.

Roles and Missions and PPBS

In its report entitled *Directions for Defense*, the Commission on Roles and Missions of the Armed Forces deftly avoided its assigned task while making over 100 recommendations, including the proposal of changes to PPBS (US, Commission 1995).

The commission was right in its approach, as summarized in the chairman's (and deputy secretary of defense) memorandum transmitting the report:

> The traditional approach to roles and missions – attempting to allocate them among the Services in the context of the Key West Agreement of 1948 – is no longer appropriate. That approach leads to institutional quarrels (as reported in the press during our deliberations) and unsatisfactory compromises (as discussed in our report). More importantly, it does not lead to achieving the Department's goals (US, Commission 1995).

Those familiar with the *doctrinal* war[1] among the services in the 1940s over defence organization, control of the budget, and roles and missions, should cheer the action of the current commission. It would have been nice if the commission had noted that PPBS has played a major role in diminishing the intensity of warfare among the military services. Otherwise, the commission might well have been stuck with yet another battle under the "rules of engagement" inherent in the "traditional" approach to roles and missions.

Long after the *National Security Act* of 1947 and the Key West Agreement of 1948, the interservice conflict continued vigorously throughout the 1950s. One of the conflicts over short-range air defence missiles, which for several years remained unresolved by a weak secretary of defense, led the Senate Armed Services Committee to initiate the practice of annual authorization of appropriations in 1959. If the secretary of defense (SECDEF) could not decide, the committee would. PPBS changed the battleground: (i) through the program structure that arrayed the decision space based on the juxtaposition of program elements that were perceived to be "substitutes and complements;" and (ii) through the analysis, recommendation, and choice of system "mixes." After 35 years of PPBS, the services remain quite willing to indulge in occasional brawls,[2] but these are nothing like the visceral strikes at the jugular vein that were common a half-century ago.

Turning to the commission's recommendations regarding decision support processes and management structures (pp. 4-8 through 4-26), directions for the future are outlined:

> We propose the following four initiatives to improve the executive and legislative branches' decision-making. Each builds on recent progress towards a more integrated and effective Defence establishment. Collectively they emphasize missions and outputs while promoting innovation and constructive competition.
>
> - Create a stable and enduring national strategy and spending plan every four years to guide DoD's planning, programming, and force development.
> - Restructure the Planning, Programming, and Budgeting System (PPBS) and other decision support processes to improve integration and provide clearly defined responsibilities for the various participants. This initiative includes strengthening the Chairman's Joint Warfare Capabilities Assessment effort.
> - Develop an integrated information framework that links inputs with outputs to better focus decision-making on mission performance.
> - Modify the DOD management structure to better support the Secretary, in particular by strengthening the Office of the Secretary of Defence's (OSD) ability to provide policy advice, analytical support, and independent perspectives.

The first bullet shifts most of the first "P" in PPBS to a *Quadrennial Strategy Review* and *mission-based planning* (US, Commission 1995, pp. 4-9 and 4-10). If this process succeeds, then attention to the *strategic planning process* would become more *periodic and very high level within DoD.*

The second bullet becomes most explicit in Figure 4-2, "Highlights of a Restructured PPBS Process (Annual Budget Cycle)," (ibid., pp. 4-11). Driven by the Quadrennial Strategy Review, planning and direction by SECDEF becomes "front-end planning" by the Office of the Secretary of Defense (OSD) and Joint Staff. The results become SECDEF direction to the services and other DoD components to prepare program and budget submissions to be subjected to an OSD combined program and budget review leading to SECDEF decisions.

These two bullets lead to the third bullet — a "mission- and output-oriented assessment framework" for use in the Quadrennial Strategy Review and the front-end planning of the annual cycle (see especially ibid., Figures 4-3, 4-4, and 4-5 on pages 4-18 through 4-20).

The fourth bullet simply stresses the proposed locus of decision — a strengthened secretary.

The changes embodied in these proposals can be expected to be exceedingly controversial and their adoption, in whole or in part, promises to generate intensive study and debate, as well as staggered implementation. There are *generic concepts* involved which stem from previous versions and developments in PPBS. For example, a "mission- and output-oriented assessment framework" is remarkably reminiscent of the "major mission and support structure" developed in the early 1970s and subsequently abandoned; the combined program and budget review was a major recommendation of the Defence Resource Management Study (Rice Report) in 1979; and, the organizational basis for the OSD/JCS dominance of "front-end planning" reflects the role of OSD in the original 1960s' PPBS combined with the role of the joint chiefs of staff since the *Goldwater-Nichols Defense Reorganization Act* of 1986.

The bottom line is that reform of PPBS may be more actively at issue than at any time since the Laird reforms in 1969.

INTERNATIONAL RESOURCES MANAGEMENT

Changes roughly parallel to those in US defence have been occurring around the world. With the end of the Cold War, many nations have been "downsizing" defence. Global trends from 1990 through 1995 are displayed in Figure 2, which is derived from data published by the IMF. In just five years, global military expenditures as a percent of GDP have declined by one-third, from 3.6 percent to 2.4 percent; industrial country military expenditures have declined by one-fourth, from 3.2 percent to 2.4 percent; and, developing country military expenditures have been cut almost in half, from 4.9 percent to 2.6 percent.

Even more striking has been the decline in arms transfers as reported by the US Arms Control and Disarmament Agency. Global trade, measured in 1994 dollars, has declined from $71.48 billion in 1988 to $22.12 billion in 1994.

As the need for new equipment has lessened, attention has focused increasingly on improvements to be made in operating costs through the modernization of business practices, especially in financial management, most notably in the United Kingdom, Sweden, Norway, Australia, and New Zealand. In fact, progress appears to be occurring more rapidly in these countries than in the United States. Meanwhile, countries in "transition" in Central Europe belatedly are in the process

FIGURE 2: Military Expenditures as a Percent of GDP

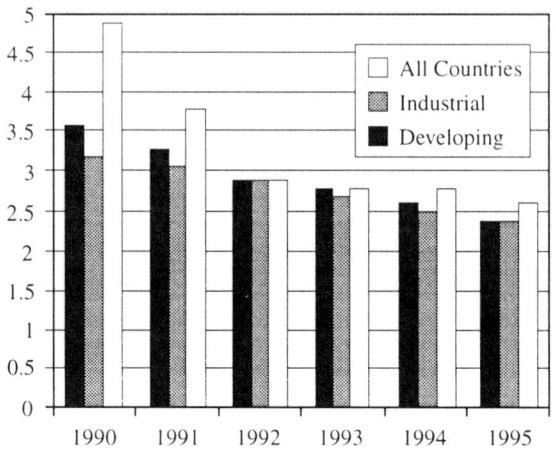

Source: IMF, World Economic Outlook database (130 countries).

of discovering PPBS. Many of the developing countries still lack strategic resource management tools. Hence, this area of instruction remains important for these countries.

CONCLUSION

The developments discussed in this paper do *not* require any radical or wholesale departures from the way defence resources management have been taught in the past. Instead, a modest shift that gives more attention to operations and less to weapons acquisition is appropriate. Economy and efficiency in collecting garbage on a base becomes a key lesson. The economic analysis of a proposal for "out-sourcing" some routine operations becomes more relevant. Managerial economics and operations research directed at daily operations merit prominence.

Cost analysis of operations deserves at least equal time with cost analysis of potential new systems. And along with these adjustments, there is also a need to offer the rationale and explain the management systems and methods of the post-Cold War era in defence resources management.

NOTES

1. Just one example of what it was like in the 1940s should make the point. General Jimmy Doolittle of the Army Air Corps, in testimony before a congressional committee in 1945, stated: "any weapon, any directed weapon that uses air as a medium of travel ... whether an airplane with a pilot or an airplane without a pilot, whether it had wings, complete wings, rudimentary wings or whether the wings are entirely absent. If it is directed after it starts off and uses air as a medium of travel, it is, then, an air weapon" (Caraley 1966, p. 81).
2. During the recent action in Iraq, cruise missiles were launched from three different platforms — Navy surface ships, a Navy submarine, and Air Force bombers. Apparently, not all air weapons are Air Force weapons. This orchestrated example, however, was not sufficient to curb the usual exhibition of service rivalry. When the Air Force was embarrassed by the refusal of Saudi Arabia and Turkey to allow the use of bases housing US (Air Force) aircraft in the region, the *Washington Post* reported that Navy officials were delighted at this setback, which proved, they believed, the value of the aircraft carrier. "The Air Force has been castrated," one Navy official crowed. "With an aircraft carrier, you get 4.5 acres of Americana with no diplomatic restrictions on when or what you can fly."

REFERENCES

Business Week, 19 August 1996, p. 6.

Caraley, D. (1966), *The Politics of Military Unification*, New York: Columbia University Press.

Hitch, C.J. and R.N. McKean (1960), *The Economics of Defense in the Nuclear Age*, Cambridge: Harvard University Press.

Perry, W.J. (1996), *Annual Report to the President and the Congress*, Washington: US Government Printing Office.

United States, Commission on Roles and Missions of the Armed Forces (1995), *Directions for Defense*, Washington: US Government Printing Office.

The Wall Street Journal, 19 August 1996, p. 1.

_____ 4 September 1996, p. 1.

CHAPTER SIX

Military Educational Reform and Defence Management Studies in Hungary

Zoltán Szenes

INTRODUCTION

Miklós Zrínyi, founder of the Hungarian military science, was the first to recognize the importance of educating military leaders in the areas of command, control, and management of military forces. His work, *Vitéz hadnagy* was published over 350 years ago. As politician, poet and warlord, he suggested that education, valor, and the experience of leadership all play equal parts in producing good leaders. Zrínyi emphasized that this training and knowledge acquisition should be done in a theoretical way. "Having a brave heart without fear is not the commander's greatest pride. His pride is not only fighting but more broadly managing an army" (Zrínyi 1985, p. 101).

Modern managerial knowledge was a long time in coming in Hungarian military education since it had been dominated by German, Austrian, and Russian philosophy and practice for the last 50 years. Officers were taught to obey the "main warlord" (king, governor, or party leader), and they were to prepare themselves to become leaders only in the pure military sense. Although both civilian and military management literature was available to civilians during the 1980s, it did not gain ground in the military schools controlled by the Communist Party, which were still using Russian teaching ideas. The disputes concerning the question of "commander or manager," which had taken place earlier in western societies, flared up in Hungary during discussions about the reform of military education only after political changes in the early 1990s. During the transformation of the education system, one of the major requirements was to bring to an end the one-party, soviet-oriented, military education and involve management training in professional military education.

DISPUTES OVER REFORM

The political changes which eliminated the obstacles to building an independent army — along with improving national defence and reforming the army in the long term — happened according to the rules of parliamentary democracy and the interests of the country. With the decline in external influences, the return to national military customs began, along with the beginnings of a movement to "catch-up" to other European military societies.

During the buildup of the national market economy, along with principles of market rationality and economic considerations, more modern methods for handling budget restrictions became important in the army's operations. After the collapse of the Eastern bloc (the Warsaw Pact), Hungary's search for security made the orientation toward NATO a top priority, resulting in the use of western-style strategies, doctrines, and procedures to improve national defence.

The tasks of democratization, transformation, and modernization of the military evolved from long political and professional disputes; and the problems and contradictions of the age were certainly present. Political decisions were made about building an army that would accept civilian control and was sensitive to society's legitimate roles, which required the armed forces to be subject to the same laws and processes as civilian society. Society needs an officer to be a citizen in uniform — undertaking professional and personal development of and dominated by professionalism (J. Szabó 1995*a*, pp. 165-96). In order to create a modern army, a new education system was necessary.

Debates concerning the changes and reform of higher education revolved around a number of problems and levels. On the political level, the question became whether the education of the military personnel should be a part of the civilian education system and expand, or should it stay within the military and continue just to provide professional military education? On the professional level, the core of the problem was the modernization of education and training. Regarding structural changes, serious disputes arose about reform, reduction, and integration of the present military institutional system.

At the beginning of the 1990s, there was a difference of opinion regarding the reform of higher education of the military between the General Staff of the Hungarian Defence Force (HDF) and the bureaucracy of the Ministry of Defence. The ministry wanted to incorporate civilian educational reform, with its democratic changes and civilian control, and to implement reform of the military university education using the rules of higher education while keeping the necessary military characteristics. The military command wanted to keep military institutions[1] under its own control[2] since this would allow it to better regulate and teach military professional goals and ideals to its students (i.e., the cadets).

The counter-arguments, doubts, unanswered questions, and fears (real and imaginary) that emerged during the talks seem to have centred around seven areas of concern: (i) the order of non-commissioned officer (NCO) training as well as the reserve command training; (ii) the future regulation of military students in the military staff; (iii) the problems of subordination and coordination of subunits providing university education; (iv) the adaptation of gradual training to the military special course system; (v) the service relationship of career officers teaching in state schools; (vi) the enforcement of regulations by the general staff; and (vii) the conversion of the double system of financing and material provision into a one-channel system. In reality, the dispute was about the right to control military education and the authority over the institutions that provide that education. The command of HDF (along with many experts) could not imagine excluding educational institutions from the force structure — placing military education under the direct control of the ministry. This would require changing the system of supervision, maintenance, and operation; in order to adapt to the requirements of the laws on higher education. The ministry along with education reformers insisted on making military education part of the civil education as a way of getting society's acknowledgement of military professional credentials and unifying Hungarian higher education. Military and defence institutions were not the only educational organizations to go through such changes. All institutions that were not state-owned (e.g., church-run, private foundations, etc.) were required to make some changes.

The arguments, which continued for over three years, were about adapting the civil university system for military education. In fact, *this became a milestone in the battle over civilian control of military education.*[3] This change in the educational system is and continues to be a huge and complex exercise, but the lack of agreement between the ministry and the general staff has created a situation where there is no legislation and decisionmakers were unable to make any resolutions for years. In 1993, *Law LXXX on Higher Education* came into force. It created a unified higher education system in Hungary, established general requirements for educational institutions and teachers, and placed universities and colleges under the control of the minister of education. This strengthened institutional autonomy, ensured student rights, gave universities the right to grant scientific degrees, and began to regulate management of educational institutions.

This new education law stimulated ideas of reform and forced the HDF bureaucracy into new decisions.[4] Approval of the idea of reform along with the practical steps of change became connected to modifying the law and creating the necessary decrees.[5]

The new regulations — even though military institutions already acted as state-acknowledged institutions of higher learning[6] — completely changed the content and organizational system of military educational institutions. The changes are wide reaching:

- Control, form, and content of the educational organizations had to be changed. The university/college requirements were now specified by law and acknowledged by Parliament, the government, and the national higher education institutions (Higher Education and Scientific Council and the Hungarian Accreditation Committee). Thus, acknowledgement, classification, and acceptance of education systems are handled by higher levels of the bureaucracy and with more professionalism. In specific professional military areas, the minister of defence is in control, otherwise institutions are placed in the hands of the university/college councils.

  In order to comply with the legal changes concerning the functioning and management of military institutions, orders were revised within the HDF involving the commanders, chief of service, and arms level. The institutional councils (university/college councils) and the management of the institutions were elected, necessary professional associations formed (Council of Scientific Degrees, Professional Qualifying Committee, and Students' Council), and new regulations and documentation for institutional autonomy were produced. Rules for the selection and promotion of university/college teachers were established.

- The system of military training had to be reformed according to the training levels, qualification requirements, and syllabus specifications in the new law. In the past, qualifications for military educational institutions had been set by the Ministry of Defence. Under the new law, jurisdiction of the national higher educational institutes fell under the Ministry of Education. The new regulations required four years of college education, one year of field-officer training, and two years of further academic training. The educational system had to be redefined, and a structure created where all levels of education overlapped.

- Educational institutions, with some exceptions, had to identify with the organizational models of civilian higher education. Elements new to military colleges and academies were adopted in order to conform to the model of civilian organizations such as the establishment of university/college branches, institutionalization of student board, and involvement in educational associations (Hungarian Rector's Conference, Conference of College Directors and Hungarian Accreditation Committee). The institutional council began to include participation on the part of students; scientific relations within and outside the institution had to be rebuilt; administrative functions such as the structure of programs, exam schedules, admission procedures, scientific training, and the conferring of degrees had to be changed; and the educational possibilities for foreign students had to be examined.

The other questions that arose concerning military education were: What and How to teach? There was relative agreement that the new training must take into account the changed political and national security situation while keeping in mind the country's socio-cultural changes, and must meet the requirements of improved military technology. The debates continue over the function of officers, their place in society, along with the historical values of the military and how all these involve the methods of education.

Given the political changes in Hungary, and in the light of international relations, Hungary's politics of security are turning toward the elements of a reliable European security system (NATO). Building an army that is ready for international cooperation is a priority, but improving the military force should not mean one-sided dependence. The current job of an officer — unlike that in the past — is to take part in the organization and preparation of the military to protect the country's sovereignty and territorial integrity as well as to lead the military effectively during both peacetime and natural and economic crises. Education is essential in aiding internal reform of the military in order to help it solve new tasks and acquire new skills. A number of requirements had to be taken into account along with the modernization of training in order to meet the improved standard of education: the increased use of divisions of labour and specializations and the increased use of technology in all fields of the military, particularly information-communication-media technology. This education must represent a new professionalism that is capable of combining historical national symbols and moral traditions with necessary human and organizational effectiveness.

The debates over the new education and its structure *were divided and intense.* There was no difference of opinion about de-politicization, about eliminating the study of Marxism-Leninism, nor about the introduction of studies in socio-political areas or politics. As well, there was agreement on abolishing the study of Soviet military doctrine (Warsaw Pact doctrine) along with the preconceived notion of the enemy and procedures of strategy and attack. The idea was that the concentration be on teaching military management not just on combat skills. Opinions differed on what knowledge was necessary for training requirements, producing several disagreements and resistance to changes in (i) the traditional educational structure, (ii) the establishment of new faculties and departments, (iii) the curriculum, and (iv) the place of military discipline in education. The various opinions and the lack of coordination between education institutes along with the adherence to the old form and content of the training slowed down the process of change.

The most heated debates were over change, reorganization, and integration of the institutional structure. By the beginning of the 1990s, it had become clear that the inherited educational capacity and infrastructure was too unwieldy and uneconomical for the modern, smaller military's needs. The modification of the education system began step by step, resulting in a more flexible organization which was better able to make decisions in areas such as training requirements, the shape of the institutional structure, and the number of full-time teachers and employees, along with a sports, cultural, and social infrastructure. During the reform, the following considerations had to be taken into account: the function, mission, and abilities of the institution and its relationship to the Hungarian army and the other "customers" (e.g., Ministry of Internal Affairs); and the possible career paths of graduates — their need for further education or retraining and the connection to civilian higher education. Provision of resources for these changes, along with the limits of enlargement, became priorities. Consideration of the institutional structure — as part of the process of democratization and civilization — had to meet the requirements of experts in the civilian defence sector, as well as the participating entities (civilian higher education, armed forces, and defence management). The newly independent financial management and the organization of international relations forced the new educational structure to become self-directing and self-governing with a close cooperative relationship with both its supervising institutions and its customers. The difficulty arose when the training was to be accredited (according to the law on higher education, all educational institutions were to be accredited by the year 2000). Necessary educational and functional effectiveness was to be reached through rapid enforcement of the requirements (see Szenes 1996, p. 3).

The three separate military institutions were united in September 1996. The National Defence University was established as a jointly run organization with four faculties (two university and two college). Engineering, supply, and finance are still taught at a separate college — the Military Technical College named for János Bolyai (see Appendix 2). The second phase of the education restructuring will further integrate the programs of the National Defence University and the Military Technical College, along the lines of a civilian higher education model (see Appendix 3). The vertical integration of the university and college has begun, creating by 1999 a single, multidisciplinary National Defence University.

The discussions and disputes have led to balance and harmony in the institutional conditions. The aims of the reform are:

- to meet the requirements of military officers for the next century
- to meet accreditation requirements
- to provide effective training
- to introduce a new educational system.

Different concepts of integration were chosen (horizontal, vertical, complete integration), providing a wide range of teaching options and flexibility (accredited college basic training, college graduate education, college complementary education, basic university education, supplementary university education, postgraduate education, defence professional education, and scientific training) in a framework that is easily navigated. As a result of these reforms, the twenty-first century will see a modern multidisciplinary National Defence University that fits the framework of civil higher education, fulfils defence requirements, and involves an effective educational structure with growing resources.

MODERNIZATION OF TEACHING

The aims, context, and structure of the new methods were worked out and formed the structural element of military higher education. The education system became the foundation of the new reconstruction. In order to modernize the training based on training requirements from the general staff, the Ministry of Internal Affairs, and institutional decisions by the Ministry of Defence, a ruling was made concerning "qualification requirements of the branches of military higher education," following the requirements of the HDF commanders along with consultation with experts.

A consensus was reached concerning faculties and branches, and the requests for formation and creation of special branches. The first stage of change has ended, leaving in place a more consistent, more concentrated, and more flexible training structure (see Appendix 4). The new ideas have modernized the present system as a result of the professional requirements for officers graduating after 2000. The demand for new training aims and programs is being met (Appendix 5). There will be two areas of science (social and technical) along with several scientific branches (technical, economical, political, and natural). (See Appendix 6.)

The aim of the new professional military is to produce an officer who fits the needs of national security, military defence, and political demands. He or she will be able to make use of a balanced knowledge of military studies, management and organizational courses, and scientific and technical fields along with the ability to speak another language (advanced level for university and intermediate level for college degree). The educational system, both the mental and material components, needs to keep the positive traditions that enable graduates to promote and sustain national historical values. Military higher education (primarily the National Defence University) will teach not only the military staff and elite, but also the entire national defence area. This professionalism shows up in the new programs that appeal to the military interests (security and defence studies, defence management), and to people outside the military such as border guards, police officers, and civilian experts.

The new training structure employs the principle of teaching civilian theoretical ideas and technical skills along with the practical knowledge necessary for military officers. Many experts, abroad and in Hungary, feel that the success of international missions (IFOR, international peacekeeping, PfP cooperation) is a result of this program.

The new system will not change the two-tiered structure already in place — with the National Defence University giving both *college* and *university* (supplementary university and postgraduate) degrees (Appendix 7).[7] Young officers who have received their college education at military institutions and have completed field exercises, meeting all the requirements, then have the possibility of returning to university to complete their professional training with a supplementary broader education. The introduction of a credit system has allowed young officers to partake in civilian higher education (Appendix 5). Students of the "open programs" (faculty of security and defence studies as well as defence management and the program of defence administration) will continue the five-year basic university education (although it is also possible to complete a two- or three-year supplementary program or postgraduate studies). Postgraduate instruction involves specialized teaching (education of civilian university graduates, scientific training, and courses that prepare students for direct military positions or special tasks — brigade field-officer courses, military education of officers drawn from civilian life, professional advanced military training, language training, and general staff training). Standards have been put in place to regulate levels of qualifications, for example, a four-year training college degree, five-year training, or two or three years of complementary university training, or a university degree. Changes are also being introduced in the professional training programs — the Military Technical College gives students a dual degree (e.g., officer-engineer, officer-economist).[8] The university degree is a single program degree — its graduates receive a *state-acknowledged military degree* (earlier military institutions gave dual qualifications — military and civilian degrees).

These changes have been motivated by the educational possibilities; by personnel and materiel requirements; and by the strengthening of the military connection through professional training and the ever decreasing number of students.

This last played a major role in the reduction of available programs (Table 1). Through the reform of the HDF through the year 2002, the number of graduating students should stabilize at around 300-350 over the long term.

TABLE 1: Graduates of Military Higher Education

Year	Education Institutes			
	MC Szentendre	AFC Szolnok	MTC Budapest	University Faculties
1989	213	94	356	172
1990	200	96	391	229
1991	135	42	240	150
1992	64	28	144	144
1993	76	-	144	172
1994*	-	-	-	72
1995	35	15	118	101
1996	79	36	185	125
Total	802	311	1578	1165

Note: In 1994, there was no graduation from military colleges.

The next step of setting up programs began, coordinated by the Higher Education and Science Council and the Hungarian Accreditation Committee. Criteria were set out for the syllabus (subjects, numbers of lessons, etc.), the military requirements, required educational backgrounds, and the funding possibilities. Finding equivalent accredited civilian faculties took time. Fulfilling these requirements were important for collaboration with already accredited programs and institutions — allowing the input of highly qualified civilian experts in areas where the military university may not have expertise.

The overview of the various training branches by the institutional councils helped solve some of these difficulties. While in the planning stages of the new system, efforts were focused on both getting approval for the documentation and applications for the new programs that were to begin in September 1997. Government regulations had to be met for educating top military leaders, border surveillance officers, and defence policymakers in both administration and management. Intellectual and material resources had to be found. It is important to define the requirements needed to establish new professional programs, to bring the debates to an end, and to concentrate on the preparation of the educational programs. This involved a long, complicated, and independent method of program formation.

The modernization of the educational system must be followed by an analysis of subject structures, contents, curriculum, and teaching documentation. The curriculum must present relevant and up-to-date information and methods and there must be an understanding of what is out of date. In updating the curriculum, the latest results of science and technological advances must be used as well as the chance to apply these advances. The contents of defence courses must be aware of both the requirements of a Euro-Atlantic connection and the use of universal (eastern/western) information. With the continuous modernization of the education system, there needs to be a balance of civil-military knowledge. Learning several languages is important for internationalization, mobility, and to meet NATO standards, while computer knowledge is important for both management and communication.

Many international organizations have offered advice and studying abroad is now a possibility. The structure of the various programs has been well studied, and parts — free choice of subjects, possibility of joint military-civil education, introduction of the credit system, methods for maintaining quality control — have been used with greater frequency. The educational system, its administration and methods of control, was changed through the use of organizational procedures.

The essential transformation of the training structure was carried out in order to focus the emphasis more on learning than teaching, and in parallel, the order of study was reorganized in order to be student-centred. Taking part in international military cooperation focuses attention on the need for a leader who can recognize and solve problems, not just reproduce information and someone who can function self-sufficiently in a cooperative hierarchy as well as take responsibility for making individual decisions. These requirements contributed to the adoption of civilian norms, procedures and teaching methods (e.g., number of classes, class-planning, semesters, etc.), along with the atmosphere, public life, and relationships of colleges and universities.

The modernization of the educational system and order of study does not mean the complete reorganization of defence education according to civilian principles, rules, and norms. In meeting the new requirements, we will also be maintaining and developing values that have accrued over the past three decades (e.g., the positive elements of a professional calling, the "soldier-like" method of organization, the increased strength of the officer training over the past half-decade, and the new specializations in the training for military police). It is essential to keep in mind the legal relationship of the students — the differences and similarities of the "officer cadet" and "university/college student," and determine the varying dimensions of the values of behaviour, attitudes, and socialization roles. This approach includes the civilian students as well, since they will be working in an area that is more regulated, more rigorous, and more specialized.

INTRODUCTION OF MANAGEMENT TRAINING

One of the main elements of the education renewal program is to add management and leadership training. Teaching military management is not new in the Hungarian military higher education, but it reflected the former Eastern-European perspective in which the military leader is first and foremost a combat commander. As such, the commander's main task was to carry out certain missions and to achieve tactical, operational, or strategic goals at any price. The individual had to be both a tactician and military leader as well as a technician and logician, and had to have both military and moral authority to meet all requirements.

Besides, he or she had to be a person with great physical, mental, and psychological strength. Thus, military leadership in wartime situations dominated educational programs; and the problems of acquiring modern management techniques and introducing them to the leadership were shoved into the background. During the renewal of the training program, western ideas of management — which state that in order to achieve organizational goals the coordination of all organizational sources is needed — are being taught. Introduction to the modern view of management was helped by the fact that in the 1990s, there was an acceptance of western literature and thinking on the place of the military in society, which stated that following a political change in the system, the relationship between the army, politics and society, and historical experience must be reevaluated and the profession must move to meet new requirements. A number of the elements of the new view of the military profession (i.e., the military profession must remain acceptable to society; only an army integrated into society can follow its growth; and only a soldier who is socially motivated and qualified in military science and leadership will meet basic requirements) strengthened the view of the importance of training military managers. This expansion in military higher education was made easier by the increased training of managers in civilian areas — financial, technical, human resources, cultural, etc. (Krizbai 1993; J. Szabó 1995*b*; M. Szabó 1993; Perjés 1995). Determining the civilian content for the diploma was not a problem for professional nor intellectual material. The tradition of military educational training and the success of this training supported the introduction of management and leadership training. Leadership training was begun in 1967 at the Zrínyi Miklós War College (ZMKA), the predecessor of the current defence university. Significant research was aimed at teaching leadership theory; cybernetics and applied military mathematics; and the analysis of problems of organizational sociology, social-psychology, and ergonomics. Unfortunately, the earlier military structure had not encouraged the study of human elements and personnel needs in management structures, nor the adaptation of modern management theories. Because of this, changes were not successful even after 1993, and only a few subjects developing management abilities were possible.

Establishing qualifying criteria for the academy education for future career officers in the various military sectors (e.g., mechanized infantry, armoured, artillery, reconnaissance, aviation) was a special problem due to the need to have a dual qualification requirement — a civilian college degree and proper military qualification. The armed forces had difficulty matching and adopting these differing requirements. Young career officers were given a general education degree and then from 1991 were granted engineering degrees. None of the solutions proved lasting: technical education became less important and leadership training lost its appeal. Then, in 1992, a change occurred that resulted in a shift to a technically oriented attitude in education, leaving no time for the study of the human science aspects of management studies.

The regulations of the *Civil Higher Education Act*, which stipulated a four-year basic university course and increased professional education in two faculties and two branches of science have precipitated a change in education toward the emphasis on management science. This was the main cause for making the decision — after many preliminary studies, situational analysis, and proposals — to develop organizational and management science into an independent branch of study within the National Defence University. Military education has changed to comply with this decision and the program of *military leadership* has been created as part of the military professional education — with a four-year academic program and an additional two-year university graduate program. The system to educate and train border-guards has been modified and a program of *certified military managers* (primarily logistics and technical) has been started.[9] A new faculty has been created for *defence administration*, meeting the needs of the broader defence sector. Defence management education has been redefined in the different military and professional courses as well as in the education of senior (staff) officers. This change in the educational structure has forced a change in the personnel, material, and technical support.

The Department of Management Science, specializing in the education of military leadership, has been established within the Faculty of Military Science. The Faculty of Management and Organizational Science combines the departments interested in managerial education, and was created in 1993. The development of departmental organizational units has occurred as a result of the changes in curriculum and education methods. (The Department of Economy and Defence Economy were joined in an effort to provide a unified program of defence economy management; the Defence Administration Department is being established; and the program of military logistics and technical management is based on close cooperation of several departments; and so on.)

The Military Leadership and Management program lasts for four years involving both branches of science (i.e., military science and management and organizational science), and includes civilian academic knowledge and professional basic training. This is the first phase of the managerial education program based primarily on college courses. Emphasis is placed on the study of mathematics, information technology, economics, law, social sciences, management science, as well as the military professional subjects. (The civilian component of the military leadership is composed of the combination of civilian technical and human resources academics.)

The second phase of the program (two-year program that begins when the officer is about 28 or 30 years of age following a field-service tour or after the fourth or fifth year of university) includes professional subject areas: military planning, management and organizational theory, process analysis, operation system development, decisionmaking analysis, defence economics, human resource management, and military logistics. Teaching of these subjects is carried out differently for each science. The first section of the program is completed by a course in military studies which is compulsory.

The goal of programs in the management departments of the Faculty of Management and Organizational Science is to train officers to be able to organize efficiently and to economically utilize logistical and technical resources, as well as to establish the necessary administrative, organizational, informational, and legal structures throughout the military (Csûrös 1995).

Thus, the programs in the second phase of the professional training include varying branches of vocational study, complementing the more specialized subjects.

The logistics part of the defence program of the Faculty of Defence Management includes the following areas of study: readying the national economy for defence measures, economics of defence, planning the defence budget, managing programs of procurement, economic law, command and control of logistics services, logistics support of operations, research and development, and crisis management.

The varying areas of study for a military technical manager include: military engineering, system technology, maintenance, specifications for military metrology, technical law, applied logistics, management of technical services, and armament support of operations.

It is seen as a nationally important initiative to have *defence administration managers* trained at a defence university that also trains personnel for civilian administrative positions, civil defence offices, civilian ministries, and the fire service. The new educational program is a special mixture of military professional skills and administrative training and meets Hungarian demands for the education of employees in the defence sector. The first three years of a five-year course involve teaching specialized subjects (mathematics, information, technology, sociology, management and organization, economics, and labour protection, etc.);

providing a strong legal grounding (constitutional law, administrative law, civil law, etc.); and complementing these with defence administration and military knowledge (defence preparations for the country, nationwide mobilization, defence economics, armed forces organizations, and law enforcement information). In the last two years of the program, a more in-depth study of professional subjects takes place (political theory, organizational sociology, management psychology, and control of home defence) along with specialized areas (the function of local authorities in defence administration, administrative law, civil law, criminal law, knowledge of civil defence, national mobilization, handling of emergency situations, etc.).

September 1997 saw the beginning of this program with great enthusiasm from students and administrative bodies. The defence management program has also been built into a program of *security and defence studies* along with a general staff officer course (similar to the war college courses). Its design is original and is based on experiences of western countries.

The purpose of the five-year, university-level security and defence program is to meet the needs of specialists in the areas of policy and defence, both in government and academics. In addition to comprehensive courses in foreign and security policy, sociology, science, the military, other languages, and international law, the future policy experts receive an intensive education in defence and security. They are instructed in management and organizational theory and civil and military command and control structure of the armed forces, with an understanding of the role of civil defence organizations during crises and war, among other courses.

The general staff officer course was reorganized along the lines of western war colleges where security policy and management studies predominate, but the preparation of military leaders ("managers using force") was not the goal. During the one-year, high-level management course, security policy strategy, military management, and command and control are emphasized. The new educational structure allows the introduction of new concepts of civil-political supervision and control of the armed forces and how to understand the role of the defence ministry. Important organizational questions are being studied.

With these changes, it is possible to formulate new ideas about future military and civilian leaders and to meld this thinking with the thinking of the general staff.

CONCLUSION

The change in higher education in Hungary has followed its own road since the beginning of the transition. The organizational framework and the contents of the new system are beginning to develop, but much remains to be done to ensure a smooth integration of military and civil education and it is essential that the education and research levels and values of the new system reach and maintain international standards.

NOTES

1. Until 1996, there were three separate military colleges and one military academy: Kossuth Lajos Military College, Szentendre; Air Force College, Szolnok; and Bolyai János Military Engineering College.
2. The colleges reported to the head of the educational institutions of HDF first and then to the chief of personnel at HDF. The Military War College was subordinate to the Chief of the General Staff.
3. It is difficult to understand the content, intensity, and length of the debate, since the "fears" that were recorded in official letters and documents concerning reform of military higher education proved to be unfounded. At the same time, many of the problems were more difficult to solve — control and autonomy, normative system of finance, military education of cadets, and the evolution of the military.
4. The political decision of 17 November 1996 on the goals, content, basic requirements, and schedule of military education reform brought about an end to the debates.
5. The major laws on higher education are: LXXX (1993), the modifications of Law LI (1996) and Law XIV (1996), which covers the legal status of teachers, students, and heads of military and defence higher education institutions. The NR138 (1996) lists all the faculties of the National Defence University.
6. After 1967, officer training schools of the HDF functioned as military colleges, and in 1985 Zrínyi Miklós Military Academy became an institution with university rights.
7. The concept of civilian higher education also uses a dual educational system. For more details, see Czinege (1994).
8. The professional content of the college education has been reformed according to the requirements of basic training at the civilian economic and technical programs of higher education.
9. The education of human resource managers for the armed forces has been carried out on a civilian university basis in a postgraduate format jointly with the Zrínyi Miklós National Defence University.

REFERENCES

Csûrös, J. (1995), "Our Remarkable Dates, Probable Overall Picture of our Future in the Educational System of Our Academy," in *Modernization of Military Higher Education*, Budapest: Bureau for the Coordination of Higher Education.

Czékus, J. (1995), "The State of Military Higher Education According to the Criteria of Law," *Modernization of Military Higher Education*, Budapest: Bureau for the Coordination of Higher Education.

Czinege, I. (1994), "The Improvement trend of the System of Higher Education Concerning the Structure and Subjects," paper on the development of higher education, Hungary: Ministry of Culture and Education.

Krizbai, J. (1993), "Commander or Manager? The Improvement of Military Management According to Western Literature," Budapest: Support Centre for Education and Culture.

Perjés, G. (1995), "A Profession Like Any Other," in *Modernization of Military Higher Education*, Budapest: Bureau for the Coordination of Higher Education.

Szenes, Z. (1996), " The Concept of the Reform of Military Higher Education," Education, *Journal of Military Science* 3: 20-25.

Szabó, J. (1995a), "How to Defend the Inevitable?" in *Modernization of Military Higher Education*, Budapest: Bureau for the Coordination of Higher Education.

—— (1995b), "The Status and Qualities of the Career Officer and the Quality Requirements," in *Modernization of Higher Education,* Budapest: Bureau for the Coordination of Higher Education.

Szabó, M. (1993), "The Experience of the Military Management Education: Theoretical and Practical Questions of Improvement," *War College Papers* 197, pp. 9-20.

Zrínyi, M. (1985), *Brave Lieutenant, The Prosaic Works of Miklós Zrínyi*, ed. T. Klaniczay and S.I. Kovács, Budapest: Zrínyi Publishing Company.

APPENDIX 1
Requirements of the Military Officer Education

Educational Aims	Knowledge	Subjects
Preparation for a general intellectual role	Age and system knowledge	sociology, political science
	Acquisition of cultural understanding	philosophy, cultural history, contemporary culture
	Communication science	foreign language, technical terminology, media, rhetoric
	Information management science	computer science, information technology
	Interpersonal skills	psychology, management theory, management skills
	Law	constitutional law, civil rights, international law, public law
Education of vocational intelligentsia (dependent on professional faculty)	Natural-scientific education	mathematics, physics, chemistry, mechanics, technical subjects
	Economic education	economics, statistics, accountancy, military economy
	Military management and organizational science	military management and organization, operating the military management systems, tactics, operational art and military strategy, knowledge of wartime law and regulations
Military socialization		history of wars, history of military mentality, history of military armament development, soldiers' uniforms and life-style, physical training, drills and firing detail

APPENDIX 2
Organizational Structure of Bolyai János Military College

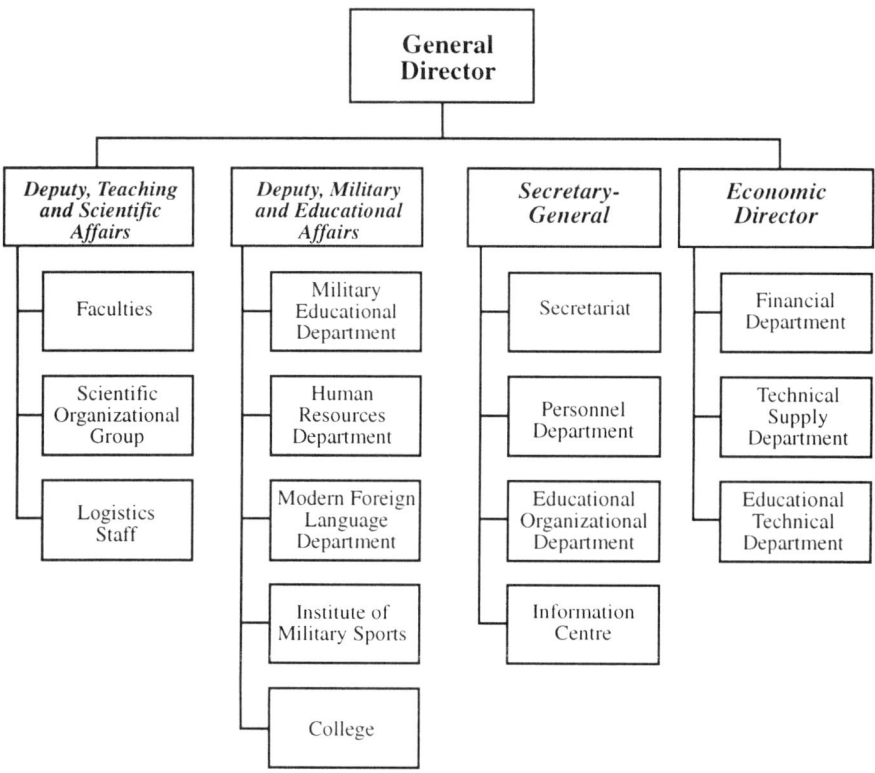

Note: Support and assistance for the military college of material equipment and logistics supplies provided by the Military NCO School in Budapest.

APPENDIX 3
Organizational Structure of Zrínyi Miklós Military College

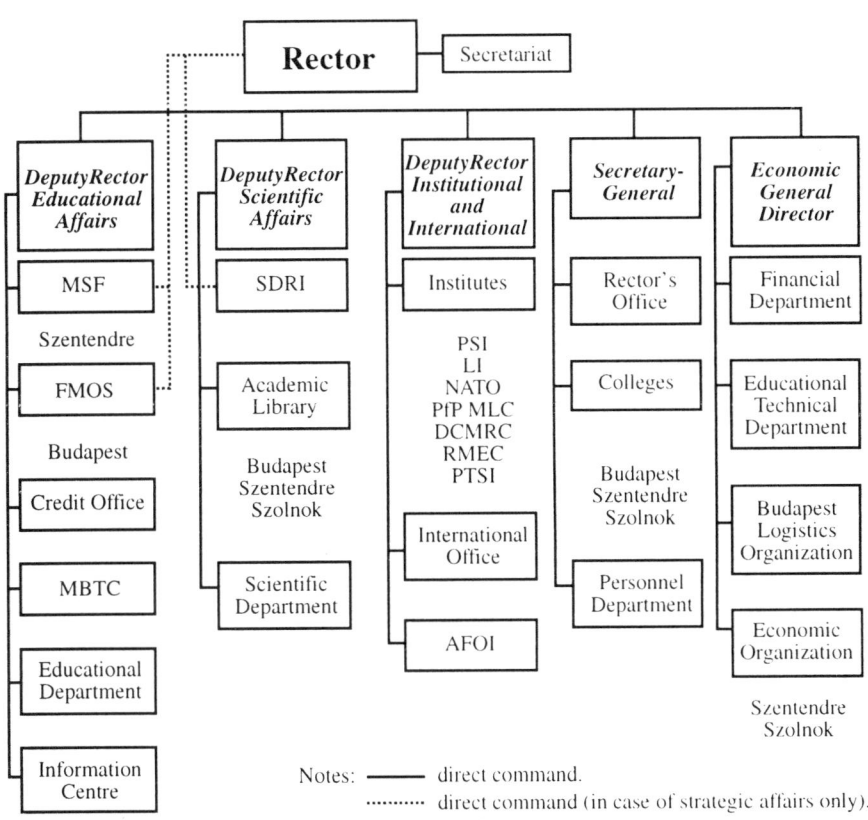

Notes: ——— direct command.
.... direct command (in case of strategic affairs only).

Abbreviation:
- MSF → Military Science Faculty
- FMOS → Faculty of Management and Organizational Science
- MBTC → Military Basic Training Centre
- SDRI → Strategic and Defence Research Institute
- PSI → Political Science Institute
- LI → Language Institute
- NATO PfP MLC → NATO PfP Military Language Centre
- DCMRC → Disarmament and Civilian-Military Relations Centre
- RMEC → Regional Military Environmental Centre
- PTSI → Physical Training and Sports Institute
- AFOI → Air Force Officers' Institute of Szolnok

APPENDIX 4
Comparison of Programs

The Name of the Faculty	
Old System	New Instructional Structure

I. University Faculties
   Military Science Faculty
   Land Forces — Military leader,
   Air and Air Defence Forces — Border policy and defence,
   Reconnaisance — Security and defence studies
   Border Guard

   Faculty of Management and Organizational Science
   Material-technical — Military logistics, military technical manager, defence administration, public security

II. College Faculties
   Szentendre
   Mechanized infantry — Military leader,
   Tank — Border policy and defence
   Reconnaisance
   Artillery
   Engineer
   Border Guard

   Szolnok
   Aviation technician
   Flight control
   Aviation pilot

   Budapest
   Air Defence Missile engineer — Mechanical engineer
   Radar engineer — Electrical engineer
   Signal engineer — Chemical warfare engineer
   Electronic warfare engineer — Information Technology engineer
   Radioelectronic reconnaissance engineer — Logistics – Economist
   Ordnance engineer — Finance – Economist
   Armour and vehicle engineer — Economics – Military economist
   Communication engineer
   Chemical warfare engineer
   Information
   Logistics
   Finance
   Economics

APPENDIX 5
University and College Qualifications

No.	Name of the Faculty	Level	Name of the Profession	Length of Course (semesters)
1.	Military command	E	Military leader (MA)	10
		F	Military leader (BA)	8
2.	Border policy and defence	E	Border policy and defence (MDA)	10
		F	Border policy and defence (BDA)	8
3.	Security and defence studies	E	Security and defence studies (MA)	10
4.	Military logistics	E	Military logistics (MDM)	10
5.	Military technical management	E	Military technical manager (MDM)	10
6.	Defence administration	E	Defence administration manager (MDA)	10
7.	Public security	E	Public security leader (MA)	10
8.	Military construction	F	Construction engineer-officer	8
9.	Mechanical engineering	F	Mechanical engineer-officer (B Eng)	8
10.	Transportation engineering	F	Transportation engineer-officer (B Eng)	8
11.	Chemical engineering	F	Chemical engineer-officer (B Eng)	8
12.	Electrical engineering	F	Electrical engineer-officer (B Eng)	8
13.	Information technology	F	Information Technology officer (B Eng)	8
14.	Security technology	F	Security-technical engineer-officer	8
15.	Economics	F	Economic officer – BSC	8
16.	Financial	F	Economic officer – BSC	8

APPENDIX 6
Areas of Military Higher Education

Scientific Areas	Branch of Science	Education Faculty
Natural Sciences and Technical Sciences	Transportation	Transportation Engineering
	Chemical	Chemical Engineering
	Technical	Mechanical Engineering Electrical Engineering Technical Information Defence Management Security Technology
Social Sciences	State Science and Jurisprudence	Defence Administration
	Economic Science	Economics, Finance
	Political Science	Defence Policy
	Military Science	Military Leadership, Border Policy and Defence, Public Security

APPENDIX 7
The Hierarchy and Connecting Possibilities of the University and College Basic Faculties

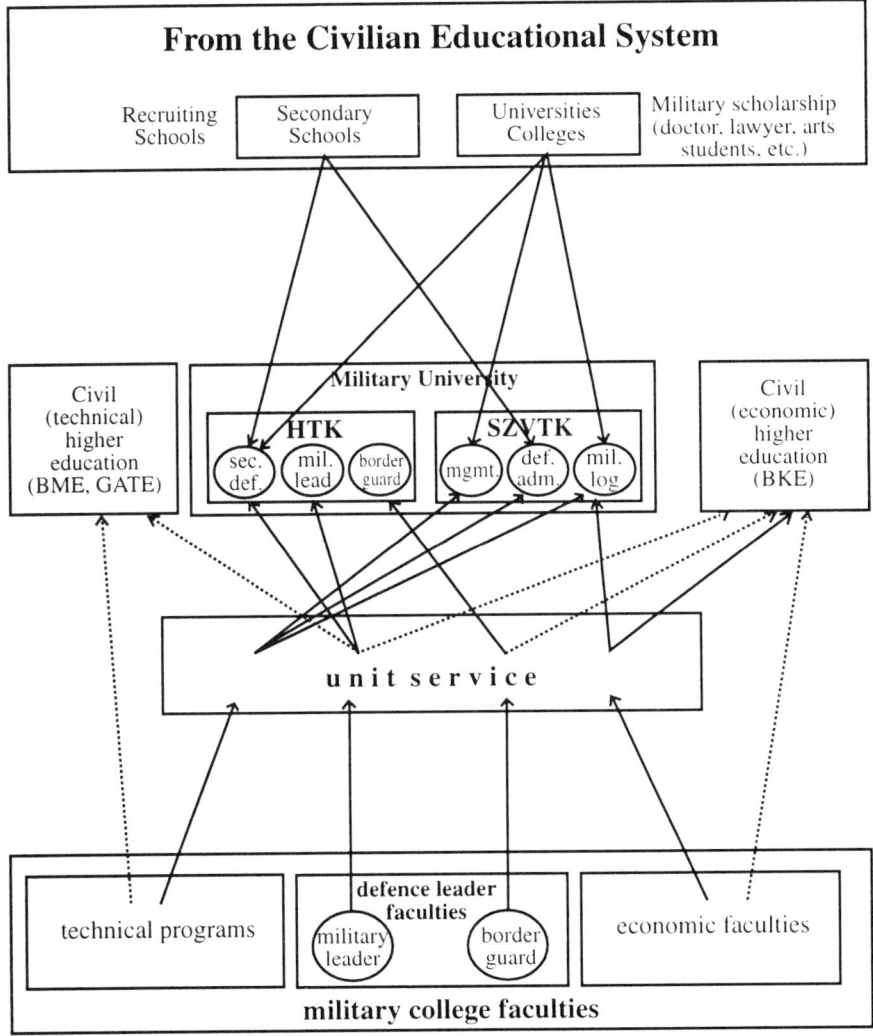

Notes: 1. The schematic shows the typical varieties of the programs (faculties) of the military higher education and the permeations between the different faculties.

2. Officers graduating from military leadership programs will have the chance to enter civilian higher education programs using the national credit system. This will follow their field service. These opportunities will arise in response to future personnel needs of the Ministry of Defence.

Contributors

Douglas L. Bland holds the Chair in Defence Management Studies, School of Policy Studies, Queen's University, Kingston, Canada.

John E. Dawson, Defense Resources Management Institute, Naval Postgraduate School, Monterey, CA.

Cathy Downes, Senior Research Officer, New Zealand Defence Force, New Zealand.

Martin Edmonds, Centre for Defence and International Security Studies, Lancaster University, Lancaster, UK.

Charles J. LaCivita, Defense Resources Management Institute, Naval Postgraduate School, Monterey, CA.

Brigadier-General Zoltán Szenes at the time was Assistant Under-Secretary (Education and Science) Ministry of Defence, Budapest, Hungary. He is now the Military Representative of the Hungarian Defence Forces to the Military Committee of the North Atlantic Alliance, Brussels.

John M. Treddenick, Professor, Department of Politics and Economics, Royal Military College of Canada, Kingston, Canada.

Queen's Policy Studies
Recent Publications

The Queen's Policy Studies Series is dedicated to the exploration of major policy issues that confront governments in Canada and other western nations. McGill-Queen's University Press is the exclusive world representative and distributor of books in the series.

School of Policy Studies

Diplomatic Missions: The Ambassador in Canadian Foreign Policy, Robert Wolfe (ed.), 1998
Paper ISBN 0-88911-801-9 Cloth ISBN 0-88911-803-5

Canada's National Defence, vol. 1, *Defence Policy,* Douglas L. Bland (ed.), 1997
Paper ISBN 0-88911-792-6 Cloth ISBN 0-88911-790-X

Lone-Parent Incomes and Social-Policy Outcomes: Canada in International Perspective,
Terrance Hunsley, 1997
Paper ISBN 0-88911-751-9 Cloth ISBN 0-88911-757-8

Social Partnerships for Training: Canada's Experiment with Labour Force Development Boards, Andrew Sharpe and Rodney Haddow (eds.), 1997
Paper ISBN 0-88911-753-5 Cloth ISBN 0-88911-755-1

Institute of Intergovernmental Relations

Canada: The State of the Federation 1997, vol. 12, *Non-Constitutional Renewal,*
Harvey Lazar (ed.), 1998
Paper ISBN 0-88911-765-9 Cloth ISBN 0-88911-767-5

Canadian Constitutional Dilemmas Revisited, Denis Magnusson (ed.), 1997
Paper ISBN 0-88911-593-1 Cloth ISBN 0-88911-595-8

Canada: The State of the Federation 1996, Patrick C. Fafard and Douglas M. Brown (eds.), 1997
Paper ISBN 0-88911-587-7 Cloth ISBN 0-88911-597-4

Comparing Federal Systems in the 1990s, Ronald Watts, 1997
Paper ISBN 0-88911-589-3 Cloth ISBN 0-88911-763-2

John Deutsch Institute for the Study of Economic Policy

The 1997 Federal Budget: Retrospect and Prospect, Thomas J. Courchene and Thomas A. Wilson (eds.), Policy Forum Series no. 35
Paper ISBN 0-88911-774-8 Cloth ISBN 0-88911-772-1

The Nation State in a Global/Information Era: Policy Challenges, Thomas J. Courchene (ed.),
Bell Canada Papers no. 5, 1997
Paper ISBN 0-88911-770-5 Cloth ISBN 0-88911-766-7

Reforming the Canadian Financial Sector: Canada in a Global Perspective,
Thomas J. Courchene and Edwin H. Neave (eds.), 1997
Paper ISBN 0-88911-688-1 Cloth ISBN 0-88911-768-3

Available from:
McGill-Queen's University Press
http://www.mcgill.ca/mqup
Tel.: 1-514-398-3750